CRAIG

"What is straight and what is hip, and what exactly was *he?* That bugged him. He wanted to be able to communicate with everybody, and it bugged him that he couldn't. The more he understood about himself and life, the harder it became for him. He used to tell me how it was important we do something for the rest of the kids in school, and help them communicate, feel more deeply. I told him that he would have to accept the fact that they weren't worth the trouble. But he couldn't think that way. He *had* to care. He *had* to try."

—Stanley Pietrowski, a friend

AND JOAN

"She was like two different people, the way everything was pulling her one way, then the other. She used to think she had to put on an act to be accepted. She thought she had to do prestige things, like being a cheerleader. That's what everybody told her to do, so she did them. She wasn't very happy at home, there was so much hassling going on between all her brothers and sisters. She was such a gentle girl, so lovely, it must have upset her terribly, but she would hardly ever talk about it. She didn't want to gripe. She wanted to find the positive things."

—Desi Worland, a friend

SOON TO BE FILMED BY
PRODUCER-DIRECTOR ROBERT WISE
AS A COLUMBIA PICTURES RELEASE
FROM THE FILMAKERS GROUP.

CRAIG
and
JOAN

TWO LIVES FOR PEACE

ELIOT ASINOF

A DELL BOOK

ACKNOWLEDGMENTS

Bibo Music Publishers, Inc.: From *Talking Atomic Blues* by Vern Partlow. Copyright © 1950, reprinted by permission of the publishers, Bibo Music Publishers, Inc. Charing Cross Music, Inc.: From *A Most Peculiar Man* by Paul Simon. © 1966 Charing Cross Music, Inc. Used with permission of the Publisher. Irving Music Inc.: From *Let's Get Together*. Copyright 1963 Irving Music Inc. (BMI) All Rights Reserved. Words & Music by: Chet Powers. Kirshner Entertainment Corp.: From *Give Peace a Chance* (Lennon-McCartney). Copyright © 1969 Northern Songs Limited. All Rights Reserved. Used by permission. Edward B. Marks Music Corp.: From *The Dove* by Jacques Brel and Alasdair Clayre. Copyright Edward B. Marks Music Corporation. Used by permission. Warner Bros. Music: From *Ballad of a Thin Man* (Bob Dylan) © MCMLXV by M. Witmark & Sons. From *One Too Many Mornings* (Bob Dylan) © MCMLXIV by M. Witmark & Sons. Used by permission of Warner Bros. Music. All Rights Reserved.

TO THE BADIALIS

The prevalence of suicide, without doubt, is a test of height in civilization; it means that the population is winding up its nervous and intellectual system to the utmost point of tension and that sometimes it snaps.
> —Havelock Ellis, *The Dance of Life*

An act like this is prepared within the silence of the heart, as is a great work of art.
> —Albert Camus, *The Myth of Sisyphus*

Something is happening here and you don't know what it is, do you, Mr. Jones?
> —Bob Dylan

CRAIG AND JOAN

INTRODUCTION

I first went to Blackwood, New Jersey, on assignment from *Seventeen* magazine, its enterprising editor, Ray Robinson, having sensed an important message to young readers. He had armed me with a clipping from page one of the *New York Times*, October 17, 1969: "BOY AND GIRL DIE IN ANTIWAR PACT. Commit suicide in Jersey after Moratorium Rally" and a challenge to "find out why; why did they do it?"

It was like giving me a camera and telling me to go and photograph the view from the top of Mount Everest.

It followed that my article about Craig Badiali and Joan Fox, the two suicides, would fall shy of reaching such a majestic peak, but there was enough meat in it to evoke an extraordinary response from the magazine's readers. The story, apparently, touched a terribly sensitive nerve in America's troubled existence. I was not surprised. By the time the article appeared, I had long since been aware of this and had plunged into the greater commitment of writing a book.

The problems were enormous. It became immediately clear that the parents of both children were completely indisposed to cooperate, their continued grief so dominating their existence that any mention of the tragedy was a source of unbearable pain. Then, too, they had suffered the pressures of a vigorous coverage by the news media during that anguished week, and anyone close to the two families could not but rebel at my presence. Above all, however, it was the essence of the story that was at the heart of their silence. In the matter of suicides, all manner of sensitivities lie trembling below the surface —especially if the political motivation behind it places a stigma on them all.

Was it possible, then, to write about the lives of two teen-agers without the active cooperation of their parents? Could I learn enough from others? Could a total stranger piece together the fabric of their lives in the face of all this resistance?

"My brother died for his convictions. They were anti-war," the *New York Times* had quoted Craig Badiali's older brother, Bernard, Jr., and it was to him that I turned for help.

He came to meet me in my motel room, openly wearing his grief about Craig and his doubts about me. Like his parents he had thought of little else since the death of his brother, but unlike them he could not suppress his need to expose his feelings. An English major at college, he had thought of writing a book about this himself—or contacting someone like Truman Capote with whom he might work, for he could not bear the torment that the beauty of his brother's death should not be known to all. In time, he came to trust our relationship, opening the floodgates of his emotions, exposing a remarkable flow of confessions and insights.

Magnanimously, his parents did not object. Indeed, they were in no way intrusive, respecting their son's needs as he respected their need to remain silent. My visits to their home were entirely pleasant. I was always welcomed and never made to feel compromised, though it had been understood that Craig would not be discussed in my presence. There was even an attempt to bring me together with the Fox family, initiated by the Badialis in the hope that we might all come together in a unity of purpose—a dinner invitation which Mrs. Fox at first accepted, then reconsidered. It was never to be. The Foxes did not wish any of the family to discuss the affair with me.

If this created a gap in the structure of the book—for Joan would not be pictured inside her home—I sought to fill it with the comments of her friends. Fortunately, there were several who were eager to participate, recreating their relationships with Craig and Joan with absolute candor. As a result, a rather full and many-faceted portrait emerged—not only of Joan but of the kids themselves. The more they exposed themselves, the more they came to wonder what I thought of them, and the roles began to reverse: they had found a new friend from "the outside world" and it was they who began to probe. If I was so concerned over the problems faced by the two suicides, did it not follow that I should be concerned about them too? I was, and so we helped each other, and by the completion of this work it could be said that all of us had learned something more about ourselves as well as about each other.

There were others who would not cooperate. Some refused to talk with me, sometimes because their parents instructed them not to. Others would arrange to meet in some furtive way, at the local diner, for example, or at a friend's house. Some would indicate their mistrust of my purposes: "What for?" they would ask. "Wouldn't it be better to forget the whole thing?" At the high school I was told that my presence had become "an upsetting influence on the children" and at one point I was politely but firmly asked to leave.

In the end, even these negative aspects of the long winter and spring became an integral part of this work. If the sensitivities of Blackwoodians precluded a complete airing of their opinions, that, too, was intriguing, for it lent the story a deeper significance. Indeed, the very forces that appeared to work so strongly to prevent its exposure served to implement its dramatic power.

It is frequently true that the pursuit of a story can be as dramatic as the story itself. It was notably so in this instance. I emerged from the experience moved and shaken, nursing a somewhat awed sense that I, too, had been party to the tragedy. I can only hope that this account will prove that it is not better "to forget the whole thing," and that however "upsetting" my presence was to anyone, it will bring about a greater understanding.

1

Mrs. Frances Badiali—or Dolly, as she was called—had always been a light sleeper with a built-in sensitivity that recorded the comings and goings of her family. On October 16, 1969, sometime around two a.m., she stopped fidgeting and left her bed completely. For over an hour she had been anxiously aware that her seventeen-year-old son, Craig, had not come home.

She had last seen him before seven when she left to visit her ailing mother. Craig, she knew, went to pick up his girl friend, Joan Fox, and from there to return to the Peace Moratorium ceremonies at nearby Glassboro, New Jersey, where a candlelight march was to take place. Since they were expected back by midnight at the latest, the one-thirty-a.m. phone call from Joan's mother had not been surprising. The parents were not permissive about this sort of tardiness, and always expected them back on time. On this night, neither child had called in to explain and neither parent could suggest where they might have gone.

Though cordial enough, the two families were not close friends, their relationship revolving around the romance of the children. There had been some talk that the Foxes were not entirely pleased by the extent of their seventeen-year-old daughter's involvement with Craig. Craig, for one, had mentioned it a few times but shrugged it off as a matter of no great consequence to either Joan or himself. As a result, Dolly Badiali had said nothing further about it, though her sensitivities were inevitably stung by what appeared to be a less-than-complimentary appraisal of her son. There was, however, no suggestion of any dissension during this late-night phone call. They assured each other there was nothing to worry about, that there must be a simple and innocent answer to the whole thing. Above all, they promised to call each other as soon as there was news.

It followed that Dolly could not go back to sleep and would make no attempt to try. The house was quiet and she did nothing that might disturb it. Her husband, Bernard, Sr., a hard-working and heavy-sleeping man, would awaken at five-thirty. Her older son, Bernard, Jr., twenty-one, was in the recently created apartment upstairs, with his wife and baby son. So she went to the kitchen, made a pot of coffee, and sat there alone, and wondered.

Craig, she recalled, seldom slept well as a baby. Seventeen years ago his crying had kept her awake through what seemed like equally endless nights, and in order not to awaken the others (her parents were living with them then), she would bring him to the kitchen on her hip while she prepared a bottle for him and coffee for herself. What was there about him that had caused such restlessness? What made him so different? The doctor had explained that it was not abnormal, that Craig was neither sick nor colicky, but probably had what they called an overactive cerebral cortex, a characteristic that sometimes indicated a potential for a higher intelligence. She would cradle him in her arms, struggling with a lullaby through her own sleepiness until he subsided, and she would sip the hot black coffee in the stillness around her.

Precisely at five a.m., as if to announce the beginning of the new day, the phone rang on the wall a few feet from the kitchen table, and she reached for it even before the first ring had run its course. It was Mrs. Fox, apparently another all-night worrier, having committed herself to waiting until the striking of the hour before calling, hoping that her own phone would ring in the interim. Their conversation was different from the earlier one only in the rising anxiousness in tone.

The call awakened Bernie, Jr., a light sleeper himself because of his infant son. Five months before, he had brought home a wife, Margaret, and a baby, Matthew, after two years at Brevard College in North Carolina, and had settled in his parents' home until he could get his degree and his prospective professional life as a teacher organized. Bernie was tall, though not quite as tall as Craig's 6'2", but leaner and more athletic in build and action. They were, however, brotherly in appearance, their straight dark brown hair, always cleanly barbered, settled the same slightly curved way over their foreheads; formidable square jaws; slightly acne-scarred complexions; and, perhaps most telling of all, an intelligent, sensitive probing look through brown tortoise-shell glasses. Bernie came downstairs and was surprised to see his mother in the kitchen, the pot of coffee already on the table. Hearing the news, he was less worried about the two kids than concerned for his mother. Indeed, the incident seemed hardly more threatening than a noisy thunderstorm.

"The chances are," he told her, "they had a flat tire and Craig had failed to repair the spare. God knows that's happened to me often enough."

To reassure her, however, he went back upstairs, dressed, and drove down to Glassboro to find them, convinced that they would return before he did.

The older son of Andrew Fox, Sr., was also named for his father. Andy, Jr., was twenty-seven, and after serving a tour of military duty in Vietnam (his younger brother, Raymond, nineteen, was there now), became a police officer on the Gloucester Township Police Force, its headquarters on Church Street in Blackwood, just a few blocks from the Fox home. Like Bernie, Jr., Andy was married and was the father of a young son. On this week in October he was on vacation, but when his mother called him early that morning to tell him about Joan's absence, he too immediately dressed and began retracing his sister's route to Glassboro.

Bernie returned around a quarter past six, having seen and heard nothing, "hoping they had gotten home in the meantime," but there was still no news of them. His father, meanwhile, had dressed for work, at first unaware of the problem surrounding his missing son. Conceivably, Bernard, Sr., might have had his breakfast and left without suspecting anything—he was foreman of a carpenters' crew working in Philadelphia, and frequently left before Craig had awakened for school—if Dolly had chosen to conceal this. In effect, it might well have crossed her mind, knowing the strength of his anger at any breach of discipline. She was a gentle and tender woman who hated the severity of father-son confrontations—even when she fully understood the need for punishment. But the drama had already permeated the household and her husband was quick to respond.

Immediately, he called a co-worker to report that he would not be in that morning, that there was "personal business" he had to attend to, adding that he expected to show up later.

They gathered around the kitchen table, the customary meeting place for all family occasions, and the speculations began in earnest.

"We came up with all sorts of notions typical of times like that," Bernie, Jr., said. "Like maybe they had gone off and gotten married. It was the first idea mentioned and we stayed on it for a while. There was more than enough background in their relationship to make some sense of it. God knows, they'd known each other long enough. Maybe five or six years. They'd been together for most of it, in and out, hot and cold, the way kids are, but they were always a twosome, and for the last several months they'd become inseparable. In fact, they'd never been so close, so important to each other. Craig would talk to my wife, Margie, and really expose the depths of his intimacy with Joan. It was really a complete relationship. They'd even talked about taking an apartment together over the past summer, but that, of course, had been out of the question."

Margie came down with the baby, Matthew, and said little. "I didn't believe they had eloped and neither did anyone else, really. My mother-in-law especially."

It was true. Craig was not the type to run off and elope. For one thing, he was too close to his family to do anything so clandestine. For another, he was essentially a conservative and responsible boy, not prone to adventurousness. It was Dolly, weary from the emotion of the endless anxious night, who suddenly shattered the unreality of their optimism.

"They've been kidnaped," she offered.

The words hung in the air for a moment and no one spoke.

"I guess we were all surprised she'd said that," Bernie said. "Mother was not the type to lean toward pessimism. Dad just fidgeted with his coffee, not knowing what to say, and I thought, well, poor Craig was going to catch hell when he got home, that much was sure, and he'd better have one solid set of excuses ready. Whatever had happened, he should have found a way of calling. I knew one thing: I'd better be around when he got back because he was going to need me to help him out when Dad got on him."

At fifty, Bernard Badiali, Sr., was a solid man of medium height, with a ruddy complexion, and thinning brown hair. His sons did not resemble him, either in appearance or personality. He was as tough and disciplined as a young soldier. He had grown up during the Depression and had gone to war at the age of nineteen, spending most of his adult life in uniform—twenty-two years as a soldier in the Air Force during which time he had married and fathered three children (the first had died shortly after birth). After discharge four years ago, he had redirected his life, developing his skills as a carpenter and demonstrating his resourcefulness as a leader, until he worked his way up to the top in a totally new field. He was the kind of man who could readily accomplish such a feat. Indeed, one sensed that he must have been an extraordinarily competent noncom, the kind of dedicated soldier who could always have been relied on, however difficult or dangerous the assignment. Even in his new field, his reputation for doing a complete and perfect job was unmatched, and to those who knew him as a neighbor, friend or relative, not one was the least surprised at his success.

He was a proud man, proud of his sturdy old-fashioned values, and, like many self-made men, demanding of others. He liked to tease and be teased by others, but when a situation warranted seriousness—such as the disciplining of his sons—he could be steadfast and as solemn as a judge.

During this morning of crisis, however, he had no
words to say or actions to perform. It was the kind of
violation that tended to unnerve him, the unknown factor,
and the family could only wonder what explosive thing
he might do when the time for anger would be offered
him.

It was not quite eight a.m. when members of both
families—Bernie Badiali, Sr., and Bernie, Jr., Mrs. Fox,
Linda (Joan's older sister)—independently of each other,
met at the Gloucester Township Police headquarters to
inform them to be on the lookout for Craig's pale blue
1962 Falcon sedan. Then Bernie remembered that one
of his aunts had a small cottage at the Jersey shore,
about fifty miles from Blackwood, and it suddenly occurred to him that perhaps the two kids had gone there.
Since there was no phone for them to report this, Bernie
called the local sheriff and asked him to check it out.
It was a possibility, though admittedly a small one, and
they did not delude themselves into believing it was anything but that. The sheriff replied that if he found them
he would call back. Meanwhile, there was nothing to do
but wait.

Debbie Gliick, Joan's friend who lived on South Drive,
a few blocks from the Fox home on Theresa Place in
the same building development, customarily picked up
Joan and walked to school with her. They had become
close friends in this last year. Debbie had been having a
difficult time, having grown up in a troubled household—
a quiet, brooding, introverted girl, not nearly as pretty
as Joan nor as appealingly vivacious. "I really needed
someone like Joan. I'd been hung up on a boy for such
a long time and it hadn't worked out. It was like I'd
been sick with it." The fact that someone as marvelous
as Joan should accept, even encourage, Debbie's friendship was almost too good to be true.

It was a few minutes after seven when Debbie re-
sponded to the ringing phone, wondering at such an early
communication. It was Joan's fifteen-year-old sister,
Ruthie, with a strange message that both she and Joan

weren't feeling very well and that Debbie need not stop
by to pick them up or wait for them at the corner.

"It all sounded so strange, I sort of guessed something
was up, and not the way she said it. I had finished dress-
ing when the phone rang again, and again it was Ruthie.
She told the truth this time. She said that Joan hadn't
come home all night, and did I by some chance know
where she might have gone."

All sorts of notions ran through Debbie's mind, not
the least of which was the furtiveness of this whole approach. So many people don't tell the truth unless it
becomes necessary for some ulterior purpose. But above
all, she felt an initial taste of fear.

"I stopped off at the Foxes' on the way to school and
spoke to Joan's mother. I didn't have any ideas, though
I tried to think of some on the way. Mrs. Fox did,
though; she started asking me some questions about
Joan, like maybe Joan had confided in me about certain
things that she kept from her parents. I could tell she
was worried that Joan had gotten pregnant and run off
some place with Craig to have an abortion or something
horrible like that. She didn't really say it, but suggested
it in a roundabout way. I told Mrs. Fox that it was out
of the question. I mean, she couldn't be pregnant, she
just couldn't be; to the very best of my knowledge, Joan
was still a virgin."

If Mrs. Fox was not convinced, Debbie could not help
that. Joan had other friends to whom she revealed con-
fidences, one of whom was a more worldly, experienced
girl named Desi Worland. It was possible that Desi knew
differently about Joan. Indeed, she might even be at the
bottom of this misadventure. Debbie thought, Why didn't
Mrs. Fox call Desi? But she also knew that Desi was
not exactly welcomed at the Foxes, and that Mrs. Fox
would not take kindly to any suggestion that would include her—even at such a troubled time.

"It was all so strange, so sudden," Debbie speculated.
"I don't know how it got into my head, but I started
crying on the way to school. I could feel it deep inside
of me, a terrible premonition. I didn't know how I knew,
but I knew: Joan was dead."

Directly across the street from Debbie Gliick's, another seventen-year-old girl, Gail Hillias, was having a difficult morning. She had awakened from an uneasy night with a rising fever and oncoming cold and decided not to go to school. She remained in bed, troubled by the memory of a dream she'd had. "It was about Craig, and how I'd written this poem and wanted to put it in his yearbook this coming spring. Last year, he'd written me a lovely poem and I wanted to do the same for him. But in my dream, he said no, I couldn't. And he said he wasn't going to sign my book again. Never. He didn't say why, but he kept saying no, he just couldn't."

Gail took this sort of thing very seriously, believing in the existence of her own extrasensory power. She had received similar foreboding messages before and they had actually presaged some ill fate for a person close to her, even death on one occasion. She had been brought up in the Greek Orthodox Church, maintaining a religious devotion to it. She was an attractive girl with a well-developed figure made all the more substantial by a love for competitive swimming. This was inspired by her father, a truck driver by trade, a dedicated swimming coach by avocation. Neither her father nor mother paid much attention to her occasional flights into such supernatural phenomena and Gail did not burden them about it.

On this morning, however, she became increasingly aware of the dreadful presentiment involved in her dream. It became so potent, she tried to attribute it to her feverishness. "What frightened me was that I don't think I'd ever had a dream about Craig before. I always take my dreams seriously, and they all seem to fit in place somewhere. I just couldn't understand why Craig refused to sign my book."

The Highland Regional High School was in its third year of existence, a red brick, two-story sprawling complex of buildings and athletic fields a mile outside of town. It stood almost alone in a broad flat setting of farmlands as far as the eye could see, just under the shadow of the Jersey north-south freeway from Camden to Atlantic City. Its thirteen hundred students arrived by

bus, car, and on foot (very few on bicycles). The parking area, one-third filled, was designed to accommodate
almost as many cars as students in what was, perhaps,
an eerie anticipation of things to come. Other than a few
Volkswagens, the cars were all U.S.-made, and most of
them sported decals of American flags. The students
dressed neatly and conservatively. Girls were not permitted to wear slacks, nor boys to wear jeans. Though
there were no specific regulations for boys on hair
length or sideburns, any deviation from conventional
appearance was vehemently frowned on. It was as if the
rebellious youth culture did not exist in Gloucester Township. As a result, it took an exceptional amount of courage for a dissident youth to attempt defiance.

One such boy was seventeen-year-old Stanley Pietrowski. His brown hair was thick and long, his sideburns
prominent, and he sported a flaring mustache. Together
with his steel-rimmed glasses, his appearance was as unconventional as was his manner. His inclinations were
artistic and his talents in that area appreciable. Indeed,
he came by his style as naturally as his highly respected
antithesis, the clean-cut "jock" who sported a crew cut
and varsity sweater. Nonetheless, Stanley was in no way
fragile. His body was muscular and it was said that if he
chose to try, he could have become a promising wrestler
on Highland's championship wrestling teams. "The coach
once asked me to give it a try. It was like asking a giraffe
to study violin."

Stanley came to Highland High in his sophomore year,
the year the school opened, having been thrown out of
the local Catholic high school for repeated breaches of
discipline. He remembered his first days at Highland as
vividly as the day he first discovered Picasso. "I walked
into the cafeteria at lunch and, looking the way I did,
all I could think of was what they were going to do to
me. They started making cracks—the usual dumb kind
of shit—and then they threw garbage at me. Real garbage. It went on like that for a few days and then Craig
came over and sat down with me. That's the way he was.
He was the straightest-looking guy in the school, but he
couldn't stand what they were doing. He said hello and

sat down with me. That's all he had to do to stop the abuse."

Early on this Thursday morning, when Stanley saw Debbie Gliick walking tearfully into the schoolyard, he was immediately solicitous. "She told me that Craig and Joan hadn't come home that night, and did I know where they might have gone. I didn't, but I couldn't see where there was any reason to get excited about it. Debbie was always very emotional. She could break into tears if a cloud passed in front of the sun. She said something about how she knew they were dead, and I told her that was a dumb thing to say."

Debbie, however, couldn't shed her fears. In fact, they grew throughout the morning, and she sat nervously through her first two periods waiting for the ax to fall. "I was in study hall, in third period, when Bernie walked in to see Mr. Di Ponziano, the teacher in charge. I couldn't hear what they were saying and I didn't look up, but I knew what it was, I just knew it. And when Mr. Di Ponziano called my name, I was shaking. Bernie wanted to talk to me. He asked me if I knew anything, like where they might have gone. I mentioned a cabin down at the shore that Craig had told me about once and Bernie said yes, he had already called about that, but I knew they hadn't gone there. I'd told Mr. Di Ponziano earlier what I really thought; I'd told him that I thought they'd committed suicide together."

Bernie was beginning to wear down. He had already covered a lot of territory and nothing seemed to lead anywhere. "I had gone to see Paul Di Ponziano because he was an old friend of mine and he knew Craig so well. I'd hoped that maybe he had heard something. I just didn't know where else to go."

Di Ponziano had heard something: Debbie's tear-ridden presentiment.

"I thought it was absurd, of course, and Paul agreed. But I was beginning to feel the first twinges of panic when I went to see Mrs. Wagner."

Diane Wagner was an extremely attractive young woman who looked more like a fashion model than an English teacher. She lived in a fine large house in the more fashionable town of Haddonfield with her husband, Philip Wagner III, an advertising executive for a large firm. It was commonly believed that her being a teacher was less a career than an outlet for self-expression and her need to contribute. She enjoyed teaching, and, because of her feeling for children, her efforts were deeply appreciated. Her contacts with Craig and Joan were in both English and dramatics, an extracurricular activity she especially enjoyed. Largely because of her efforts, so did Craig, recently chosen to be president of the Artisans, the Highland dramatic society.

There was nothing particularly surprising about Bernie Badiali's sudden appearance in her class. He was frequently employed as a substitute teacher in the Gloucester Township school system and was a familiar figure around Highland High. She had not yet heard about Craig and Joan's disappearance, nor even the fact of their absence from school. Though she could not explain why, when Bernie left, she felt trapped by a gnawing anxiety that something *had* happened to them, especially after hearing the reactions of Debbie Gliick, preposterous though they were. She found herself submitting to them, deeper and deeper into a morbid awareness of disaster, until finally, she excused herself from her class and hurried to Di Ponziano's room to catch Debbie before the period ended.

For Debbie, questions were one thing; it was quite another when Mrs. Wagner literally pulled her into the hall. "She seemed so worried," Debbie said, "I started to cry again. All morning, I'd been afraid all by myself; suddenly there was Mrs. Wagner and when I said the word 'suicide,' it was awful. I mean, she turned pale."

Bernie returned to the Gloucester Township Police headquarters, just a few short blocks from the school. His father, Mrs. Fox, and her daughter Linda were still there, waiting around for want of a better place to sit, and the speculations began again. "I knew Linda well," Bernie said. "We'd been to school together at Triton High, where we all went before Highland was built. We'd been in the same gang pretty much until recently. We talked about a snipe hunt that the kids had gone on several weeks before. The story was Joan had suggested it one day as a sort of joke on a few of the kids, and it had developed into a big party. There were a lot of pretty thick woods back there—it was an isolated area a few miles away that everyone called Bloody Bucket Road—and it could be they'd gone back there and maybe gotten lost or stuck. So we decided to go, Linda, Ruthie, and I. . . .

"We left the city hall and swung down Church Street, and on the way, we passed a patrol car going in the opposite direction. I spotted Andy Fox with another police officer, and they were turning into Theresa Place where the Foxes lived. I thought, God, I had to turn around and follow them. It was the way Andy looked, I think. It was all there for me in that instant, and a wave of terror shot through me. It was terrible. I caught up with them outside the Foxes' house and the bottom dropped out of me. I guess I wasn't as rational as I should have been, but I couldn't help it. All through these last hours, I'd been holding it in, my fears, the way those fears had kept growing, I knew it was going to be worse than anything I'd ever known. I charged at the officer with one thing on my mind: 'Are you sure it's them? Are you sure?' He said yes, yes, though I already knew by his look that it was so. I had to know what had happened. I had to know it all. I looked toward Andy with his bowed head; he could barely talk. They had just come back from Bee's Lane, he said. Then he told it all to me, very straight, and it was the most horrible thing I'd ever heard in my whole life."

2

On Somerdale Road, beginning at the Old Black Horse Pike at Chew's Landing—a section that dates back over three hundred years of American history—there are a number of old homes fronting on spacious farms, though since the end of World War II, hundreds of spanking new homes with neatly curving streets have sprung up in place of vast acres of corn and tomatoes and beans. A few old families have remained to resist the change, rigorously fighting to maintain their farms and the old way of life. Their farms bordered the sprawling new tract homesites, shrinking steadily in number as they fell to the enriching temptations of ever-rising land values. meanwhile, the streams and springs from which they drew irrigation have been tortured by the earth movers until they became shriveled and muddied beyond use.

The oldest of these remaining farms was owned by a man named John Bee, and the narrow dirt road that ran along the Big Timber Creek that bordered his farm was called Bee's Lane.

A farmer named Howard Anders drove by John Bee's farm around eight-thirty on this Thursday morning and noticed a light blue car in the distance, under the buttonwood trees. Partially covered with leaves that clung as a result of the morning mist, it seemed abandoned and he paid no attention to it. It was only when he chanced to meet police officer Joseph Reichert, riding patrol, that he made mention of it.

Officer Reichert had been informed by headquarters of the missing kids and immediately went to Bee's Lane to investigate. The blue Falcon did, at first, seem abandoned, its windows rolled up and strangely dark as though a shade had been drawn inside. It was only when

he opened the door on the seat across from the driver
that he saw them.

Two young bodies lay crumpled against the left side
door, covered with a layer of black carbon soot from
the exhaust of the filthy engine with a history of over
sixty thousand miles. Propped against the back seat were
two guitars, and on the dashboard, a pile of sealed airmail envelopes.

There was no doubt about it: they were dead. Immediately, Reichert called in to headquarters to report it,
as calmly and professionally as he could, though not
without awareness of its drama. Not only was the girl's
brother on the force, the chief of police, Captain Dave
Jones, was related to the boy's family.

Several patrol cars were immediately dispatched to
the scene, and the county medical office at nearby Lakeland Hospital was informed. From that office, one of the
three elected corners (or medical examiners, as they
were called under the new New Jersey law) would be
notified.

Thomas Daley received the call from Lakeland a few
minutes before nine, reporting two deaths in a car out in
Chew's Landing, and was instructed to call the Blackwood police for details. "This system may seem a little
indirect and unnecessary," Daley said, "but it was designed to avoid police collusion with a coroner that
might give a favorite an advantage and open the door to
graft. So we don't get direct calls from the police; it all
filters through the office at Lakeland Hospital."

Daley was a mortician by profession, though he appeared to be anything but. He was a good-looking man
in his mid-thirties with black wavy hair and a sporty
manner. He dressed well in bright expensive suits that
made less of his expanding paunch. In fact, his entire
style made him seem more like a successful young in-
surance executive than a man who dealt exclusively with
death.

"The bodies were covered with carbon soot. The whole
interior of the car was black with it—the two guitars in
the back, the letters on the dashboard, the windows—you
couldn't see in or out except where the boy's head rested
against the glass and blocked the flow of soot. When I

pulled his body out, I got my new sharkskin suit all dirty."

There was no doubt about the cause of death: carbon monoxide poisoning "obvious because of the cherry red discoloration of the skin.

"There were Blackwood police all over the place, even a tow truck waiting for me to finish so they could move the car [which had long since run out of gas]. Then there was this pile of letters. They were sealed, addressed to friends and family and others. I put them in my car and took the bodies over to the county medical examiner, Dr. Louis Reigert, in Pennsauken."

All this the sheriff reported to Bernie Badiali outside the Foxes' house.

"The thought of my brother committing suicide smothered me. I couldn't stay with it. He was dead, he was dead. That was horrible enough, but I could understand that. I mean, I could see how it might be possible to cope with that, how even my parents might be able to take that. But this suicide thing, that was different, like it came from another world. It didn't make sense. I couldn't see how it would ever make sense.

"My chest—it felt as if there was a ton sitting on it, crushing it, crushing the life out of me. I couldn't breathe. I remembered that my dad was at the police headquarters, and though it was just around the corner, I didn't want to be there when he found out. I drove to my aunt's house, knowing that no one would be home at that hour, and right off, I called our family doctor, Dr. Fessman. I wanted to get sedatives, especially for my mother, but I broke down on the phone. I couldn't speak. For what seemed like a terribly long time, I couldn't get any words out. Finally I told him. I asked him to come to the house, I was sure he'd be needed, but he said he couldn't, there were too many patients in his office. Instead, he would get the pharmacist to send over the sedatives.

"I drove straight home, frightened out of my head what my mother would go through when she heard the news. Then, as I pulled up to my house, my dad, the druggist with the tranquilizers—we all arrived at the same instant. We met outside the house, and I paid the druggist, but we didn't go in. My dad and I, we couldn't face going in. He was crying. He was breaking down; for the first time in my life I saw it happen. He kept asking: 'What have I done wrong? What? What?' And then, somewhere in the midst of his anguish, this other thing came out, the self-pity thing: 'What did I do to deserve this?' He said it and it made me feel terrible.

"Then, finally we went inside to face Mother. She heard us and came into the living room, and when we told her, it happened, this really horrifying thing: she broke down in a way that was worse than I expected, even. Shrill, tortured, frightening. My wife, Margie, was standing there with the baby. I grabbed the baby and took him to my aunt Pat's house next door. When I came back, my mother was still standing there. I hugged her and helped her to a chair. She was hysterical, crying, sobbing, gasping. . . . 'Yes, take the baby, take the baby . . . I'll ruin him too!' as if it were all her fault.

"It was an unbelievably terrible scene. My father, he went wild with it. You think your father is the strongest thing in the world, then all of a sudden he's not there to lean on. He's asking *you* for support. I could hardly believe a thing like that could happen. It was just because, at that moment, I wasn't crying, I guess, when everyone else was.

"My wife said to me: 'You're going to have to handle a lot of this yourself.' I was twenty-one years old, married, a father. I was supposed to be a man. But this was so horrible, I didn't know how I could get through it. Just the business with my parents, even. I hadn't *begun* to think about Craig. I mean, why did he do it? The thing was so painful, no one had said anything about that."

Around ten o'clock that morning, the press first heard about the tragedy. What with all the action around the Gloucester Township Police headquarters, especially since those offices were located in the basement of the city hall itself, there was no way to keep the news from spreading. First to learn of it was Carleton Sherwood, a young reporter from the Blackwood *Observer*, a weekly newspaper (unfortunately for the timing of the suicides) published on Thursdays and already in distribution.

Sherwood knew several members of the local police and quickly gathered the available details. Advised that the families would not be receptive to any questioning at this time, he chose to get whatever story he could through the Highland Regional High School, where teachers and friends of the pair were apt to be more communicative.

The school administration, however, was anything but. No sooner had Sherwood entered the school building and reported the news to the assistant principal, Mr. Keegan, then he was herded into the inner office to be kept completely isolated from the faculty and students. The principal, Mrs. Virginia Forneron, was determined that the school be kept totally in ignorance of the tragedy for as long as possible, hopefully until the three-p.m. closing. She did not wish the school day to be disrupted in any manner.

The leading newspaper in Camden County was published in the nearby city of Camden, the *Courier-Post*, part of the Gannett chain. Rushing to meet its early afternoon deadline, two young reporters, Andrea Knox and Thom Akeman, got on the phone and began calling Blackwood officials, county medical examiners, and even the families of the deceased. In this way, they managed to piece together only the barest of facts, none of which made up much of a story:

Two lovely, popular, seemingly well-adjusted teenagers, long-time sweethearts, clean-cut, good students (though not exceptional), the girl a cheerleader, the boy head of the dramatic society, no history of unorthodox behavior among teachers, friends, nor any special conflicts at home of the Romeo-Juliet tradition.

Akeman was immediately sensitive to what was missing: an explanation of the tragedy.

Why did they do it?

County Medical Examiner Thomas Daley brought the bodies to Dr. Louis Reigert at the morgue, where autopsies would be performed. As was his custom, then, he checked his telephone answering service and learned that newspapermen were already in pursuit. He excused himself as quickly as he could and returned to his office on

South 27th Street in Camden. He barely got inside the
door when the phone began ringing. It was Akeman from
the *Courier-Post,* wanting details.

Daley told him exactly what had happened—the
parked car on the dirt road, the vacuum cleaner hose
connected to the tail pipe, then passed through a hole
drilled in the floor of the back seat, the asphyxiation, the
bodies dead approximately twelve hours when found that
morning.

Then he let the unknown cat out of the bag: "They
left twenty-four suicide notes," remembering as he said
this that he still had those notes in his pocket.

"What!" Akeman all but leaped into the phone. "What
did they say?" he asked.

"I haven't read all of them . . . but the gist of them
was that they did it in hope for peace in the world."

Akeman was young, barely twenty-five, a few years
out of college (University of Illinois), but his mind was
sharp and he had the instincts of a good newspaperman.
There were those who felt he did not have the hard-nosed
look of a reporter, for his youthful, roly-poly, spectacled
appearance belied his aggressiveness and his ambition.
In his plans, for example, the *Courier-Post* was to be
merely a steppingstone.

When he heard what Daley had to tell him, he knew
at once that this was an important story. When two non-
descript kids commit suicide—even young lovers—it's a
local story. If the parents are well-known in the community (banker, doctor, local official), the news will get
quick coverage, probably page one, and that will be the
end of it. But this was far more commanding. The entire
nation had been stirred and shaken by the Moratorium
demonstrations on the previous day, and now two fine
young kids had apparently killed themselves to dramatize
the importance of the day. No drugs, no wild hippie-
radical-long-haired rebels.

Peace suicides?

In a town like Blackwood, he sensed what that was
likely to mean, especially to the families. But he determined to get a statement. He began dialing the Fox and
Badiali phone numbers, and kept getting busy signals.
He kept dialing until, finally, the phone at the Foxes' was

cleared and a neighbor answered. Akeman introduced himself and his paper, then asked if the family would be willing to make a statement. They would not, was the reply. No statement of any kind. Failing again with the Badialis (was their phone off the hook?), he jumped in his car and drove hurriedly to the community known as Hilltop and the neat, well-cared-for house on Keystone Avenue.

"It was some time before the dead boy's brother would talk to us. They were all obviously too far gone in grief to say anything. But he did, finally. I mentioned the fact that there were letters. He didn't seem to know about that. I asked him if he thought his brother's death was related to the Moratoriums and the war in Vietnam. He thought about that and then he said yes. 'My brother died for his convictions. They were against the war.' "

That was all Akeman needed at the moment. It was, in effect, the stuff of nationwide consequence.

Yes, peace suicides.

Thom Akeman and Andrea Knox filed their story for the Thursday afternoon edition and Akeman immediately drove over to Daley's office above the mortuary. He wanted to get his hands on those letters, knowing that if he could quote them, his follow-up story would be all the more exciting.

Daley's apartment was also partly his office, most of his contacts being conducted over the phone or on personal visits. The large living-dining area turned L-shaped into a spacious four-seat bar adjacent to which he kept the tools of his hobby: a half-dozen rifles and shotguns, eight pistols, bayonets, knives, most of which were encased in a glass-enclosed rack. He was, in fact, planning to leave that very weekend to go on a hunting trip to Portage, Maine, to a small island in the northern regions, and it began to worry him that with all this mounting hoopla he might be detained.

Yet he could see that this pair of suicides was special, how it would be newsworthy with all the peace demonstrations going on. "I've pulled bodies out of rivers that were dead for weeks. I see bodies every day, in all conditions, some real gruesome, I assure you. Usually, I don't give much thought to who they are or the circumstances of death. I just do my job, do what I'm supposed to do. But with these two kids, I guess I did feel something. I mean, they looked like they were nice clean kids. You could tell by the way they were dressed and all. I thought, it was too bad it was them and not a pair of hippies. We didn't need any more of those longhairs around, did we?"

Daley was not a medic but a mortician. "I guess I always wanted to be in the mortuary business, ever since I was a kid at my grandmother's funeral when I was impressed by the funeral director's beautiful dark blue suit; and when I saw his shiny black Cadillac, it really got to me. When I was seventeen, I was about to go into the Marines, but at the last minute I heard about a job as an apprentice at the Henry Leonard Mortuary in Camden, so I went to work there instead. At twenty-one, I went to study mortuary science at Eckles College in Philly, a one-year course, and I became licensed after passing the exams. Then I was drafted. I spent two years in Germany and France, working with the Graves Registration Unit. I was an embalmer in Germany. The army requires a harder embalming technique than we use in civilian life, stronger fluids to see to it that the bodies last longer. It was a big job. There were over three thousand deaths a year in Europe among United States service personnel. During the Berlin crisis when I was there, eighty per cent of the deaths were violent, even though there was no armed conflict. Suicides, homicides, accidents. I guess everybody got pretty nervous.

"When I returned home, I bought out my employer's place, and this apartment over it. It was a good neighborhood for a mortuary, lots of old people around here, a much higher death rate than in the new development areas. But then, there was a lot more competition. To make a decent living, I worked as an embalmer for eleven other morticians. It takes about ninety minutes to embalm a body. It pays about twenty-five dollars or so; if there's been an autopsy, thirty-five dollars. I've done so many, it's routine for me. I turn on the TV in my shop downstairs and go to work on the body. . . .

"It's a good life, I guess. My wife works for the telephone company so we both keep busy."

There were several people around Daley when Akeman and Andrea Knox arrived, including some other reporters. "You could see he enjoyed the attention,"
Akeman noted, "not that I blamed him. We kept asking
him about those letters until finally he pulled them out,
a whole stack of them, light blue airmail envelopes."

He fumbled with them, not at all sure of what he
ought to do. "The reporters were swarming all over me,"
Daley said. "They were very demanding; they even began to grab for them as if they were public property.
I had all I could do to pull them away. They wanted
to know: were they going to be given to the addressees?
I told them I didn't know. It wasn't my responsibility. I
was going to turn them over to the authorities."

The *Courier-Post* photographer took a picture of him
holding the letters, and somehow, in the confusion of
the afternoon, managed to separate from the pile one of
the notes addressed, simply, "Why?"

Akeman read it quickly, and immediately saw the
singular beauty of it. He spread the two pages out on the
table and had it photographed, the quickest and safest
way to have its contents secured.

> Why?
> Because we see
> that people just
> won't do and say
> what they feel,
> and you can't just
> tell someone to.
> It seems that
> people are only
> touched by death
> and maybe people
> will be touched
> enough to look into
> their lives
> and if just one
> person is touched
> enough to do
> something constructive
> and peaceful with

their life then
maybe our death
was worth it.
    Why—because we
love our fellow
man enough to
sacrifice our lives
so that they will
try to find the
ecstasy in just
being alive.

                    Love and peace,
                    Craig Badiali

3

Craig Badiali was born in Blackwood and lived the first four years of his life in a small house on Empire Avenue. His father was stationed at Hickam Field in Hawaii and the family moved there for a year. Dolly returned with her two sons and moved in with her parents in the house on Keystone Avenue where the Badialis currently reside, awaiting the return of Sgt. Badiali at the approaching completion of his tour of duty.

Joan Fox was from Philadelphia, part of that large migration to the suburbs in the 1950s when working people made enough money to free their families from the sinister decay of city life and its expanding black ghettos. The Badiali family (both sides of it) had been in the area for several generations and thought of themselves as "country people." Theirs was the first house on Keystone Avenue in the scenic Hilltop area above the Black Horse Pike, when the view was expansive with farmlands and grazing cows and fruit trees. They were, in many ways, different from "city people" like the Foxes in the new gingerbread tract houses that were mushrooming all over the area. Yet the transition of their life styles was inexorable, and at the time of the suicides, there was very little difference between life on Keystone Avenue and on Theresa Place, where the Foxes lived.

Indeed, when one thought of the children, there was no difference at all. At seventeen, it would be difficult to tell who had come from the city and who had not. They had, for the most part, grown up together, and at the time of their deaths, the influx of the new had so far transcended the dwindling traditions of the old that the area had become part of that common American subculture known as suburbia.

The heritage of Bernard Badiali, Sr., is Italian. His father, like so many immigrants of the 1920s, came before the rest of the family to make a place for them in the New World. An enterprising importer-exporter by vocation, John Badiali made his way to the coal regions of Pennsylvania, where he bought a boarding house that the entire family would run.

Bernard was the seventh son, a noble creation in the Italian tradition, and it could be said that his personality was inspired by the demands it placed upon him.

After growing up in South Jersey, where the Badialis had become farmers, Bernard, at nineteen, went into the United States Army. He was stationed in Panama when World War II broke out, spent the war years in England, then France, working in G-2 (Intelligence) as a skilled enlisted man.

When the war ended in 1945, he came home to see his parents for the first time in seven years. He had been stationed in a dozen countries and seen more of the world than any twenty-four-year-old had a right to expect. He met "Dolly" Ivins at a local club, a tavern where young adults gathered to drink and dance to live music on weekend nights. They were married within a year.

The Ivins family was considerably different from the Badialis—descendants of a mixture of Dutch, English, French, with generations of interbreeding among national and ethnic groups. Dolly's mother, for example, swears she's part American Indian. According to Bernie, Jr., there is also some Jewish blood in their heritage, though it is not generally admitted. The family has a history of at least four generations in America.

Dolly Ivins' father, Jesse, came to Gloucester Township from nearby Camden. He was a carpenter, dry-wall contractor, sheet-metal worker, shipfitter, and he was expert at all of these trades. As a result, he became a crew-boss with the reputation of completing jobs far quicker and better than his competition. During the war, he was called to take a work crew from the Philadelphia Naval Yard to a New York shipping center, where he was sent to Rio de Janeiro to repair an important ship.

There are those who so respected his talents that they were always amazed that he did not become a very rich man.

Jesse Ivins fathered eight children, and all of them lived their entire lives in and around Blackwood. His four sons all became tradesmen, union members in Philadelphia. Bernie, Jr., speaks of the Ivinses with great affection: "They are hard-working people, but they know how to enjoy themselves. Good plain fun. Two of my uncles even play golf. Two have bands. They are all musically inclined, especially my mother, who used to sing in a group called 'The Melodies,' sort of like the Maguire Sisters years ago. My father objected to her pursuing this, not appreciating night clubs and all the related problems. The show-business environment did not seem respectable to him, so she quit.

"My uncle Elwood Ivins, for example—he's a fabulous guy and real close to us. Though he's not well-educated, he's very intelligent. He's a marvelous husband and a devoted father, working hard to put his son through college, the kind of man who struggles to rise above his background. He has a band and he's a fine musician and master of ceremonies. He's an excellent carpenter as well, like his father, but refuses repeated offers to become a foreman. He doesn't want to be a chief, he says; he'd rather be just an Indian.

"He treats me like an adult. Friendly, respectful. We used to joke with him, like call him up to say that Ed Sullivan just called here to request his band for the Sunday TV show the following week . . . and Uncle Elwood would say, 'Call him back for me, will you? Tell Ed that I'm sorry, we can't make it; we have a previous engagement at the Chew's Landing Hotel Tavern.'

"Uncle Elwood used to be Craig's favorite, too, especially since he lived next door and was so musical. But the others are nice, too. Al, Jesse, Bob . . . and all the aunts from the Ivins family. We see them quite often. We'd sit around on the grass, play guitars, sing. I could even bring my date along, it was so friendly. We'd sing the old standard songs, country Westerns, but always with a certain style that made them come out fresh. We enjoyed those gatherings.

"My father's family, on the other hand, are distant by comparison. There's an air of aloofness about them. . . ."

Bernie, Jr.,'s grandfather Badiali, for example, died when Bernie was three, and the widow lived with one of his father's uncles. Before leaving the mining region of Pennsylvania, Bernard's oldest sister, Mary, buried two of the Badialis' fourteen children there. She became a waitress when the family moved to Marlton in South Jersey, elevating herself to a job at the luxurious Belle-vue-Stratford Hotel in Philadelphia. She was more than simply a waitress, however; she was extremely ambitious and hard-working, and after the frustrations of serious marital difficulties, began to direct herself toward a study of Scientology. Typically, her involvement was so great, it became upsetting to others, especially her brother Bernard. Her visits were seldom without extensive preaching on the subject, a fact that troubled Bernard, who could not agree with this doctrine.

"She even went to England to study," Bernie, Jr., noted. "Dad thought it highly unorthodox for a woman in her middle forties to become involved in such a 'radical' organization.

"There were few close ties in my father's family—which is rare among Italians—though they lived close enough to each other. Years ago, when they got together, they would speak Italian, several of them having been born in Italy, adding to the mysteriousness. My dad seldom talks about them now, or even about this phase of his background. He is so completely Americanized, other than his name, one would never know he was so close to that heritage.

"It followed that he would have problems with new arrivals in the neighborhood—quite a few Italians who left South Philly for a better life out here. They brought with them their old ways, their heavy accents, the way they dressed (very sharp and citified). They tended to be clannish and mistrusting. It was hard to be neighborly with them and, inevitably, my father resented it."

When Bernard married Dolly Ivins, he moved into the house on Keystone Avenue, sharing it with her parents. In order to make more room, all the carpentry skills of the Ivins family were immediately made available to the couple; Bernard was deeply impressed with their complete willingness to help.

The house was well-built and compact. Two floors, plus a basement and an attic. The roof would be raised, walls would be torn down, rooms rearranged several times over the years to keep pace with the shifting needs of the growing family. The work would be done rapidly but with love, and every change seemed to bring about a feeling of improvement in appearance and livability.

The first Badiali baby was born in the year after their marriage, only to suffer a tragic death a week after birth. Bernard, Jr., was born in 1948, then Craig, four years later. The father, having registered in the Air Force reserves when a tour of duty ended after the war, was suddenly recalled for the Korean conflict, and he began a tour of the world that took him through the Far East and South Pacific, covering fourteen years and over thirty countries. He would return home on furlough periodically; one year his family joined him in Hawaii, but for the most part, the two boys grew up without him.

It was, then, something of a jolt when his retirement came through and he returned home permanently. He had lived so long as an absentee parent, as it were; now he had to head his family on a far more realistic basis. As a father, his presence was immediately established. He loved both his sons, always had, and out of his love came his demands, many of which were right out of army traditions: shined shoes, neat clothes, frequent haircuts, a general tightening of discipline and responsibility. He was a man of the old school: when he told his sons to do something, he expected it to be done without question.

As it turned out, it was tougher on Craig than it was on Bernie, Jr. Bernie was closer to his father's image of an ideal son: tall, lean, athletic—a high school football and baseball varsity man, an excellent swimmer. At thirteen, Craig was stout and thought of himself as clumsy. He was more inclined toward the esthetics of

music and poetry, prompting those who knew the family
to liken Craig to his mother while Bernie was more like
his father.

Nonetheless, it was a warm and comfortable home.
Whatever frictions and hostilities existed in the wake of
these diverse personalities, they were experienced in a
setting dominated by love. Craig could understand his
father's sternness, even when it was directed against him.
And if there were times when he felt he had to defy it,
the defiance never went so far as to create any fundamental challenge to his father's authority. The father,
meanwhile, was not incapable of compromising his own
rigidity, bending frequently to the expanding needs of
his growing sons.

As Bernie, Jr., put it: "Our house was the kind that,
if you came home all perky and alive, you'd get challenged. One of the other men was sure to take you on
in one way or another. But if you came in looking depressed, everybody was immediately there to pick you
up."

There was no question but that it was a father-domi-
nated home. Bernard, Sr., was the kind of man whom
others respected. There was power in his style, his rugged, athletic-looking, compact one hundred and seventy-
five pounds, his sloping shoulders and flat stomach, even
in the way he looked at you when he spoke. The Ivins
brothers, for example, were considerably impressed by
him. He was always accepted as a leader.

Though he was not a simple man, he lived simply. He
rose early, at five-thirty a.m., and returned home usually
before five p.m., then showered, changed his clothes, and
relaxed in the living room with the paper. He was a
man of few hobbies: he would bowl one night a week
with the church league, though not with any special passion, motivated less for pleasure than because it was a
proper thing to do. On evenings and weekends, he
worked in a local realty office, in anticipation of getting
a license and practicing. Some evenings he'd spend at the
Freemasons' Lodge. He ate dinner with his family
promptly at six, insisting that his sons sit up straight, eat
properly, and when finished, politely excuse themselves.
The meals, cooked by his wife, were simple and whole-

some: pork chops, mashed potatoes, greens. Meat, starch, vegetable. For dessert, rice pudding, jello, or home-baked cake. Tea or milk. After dinner, he would sit in the living room with them, chat for a while, then before long, he would tumble into bed, exhausted.

"Life has been good to me," he would say, thoroughly convinced that this was so. He had struggled all his years, both in the service and out, recently arriving at that point where he could taste the fruits of his efforts, and he rejoiced in the awareness that it had all been worthwhile. He was a man who could suffer tragedy and still count his blessings, knowing that life was supposed to be no other way and that it was up to the individual to make the best of whatever he had to face. His was an old-fashioned orientation and, as Bernie put it: "Most kids, like some of Craig's friends, would consider that sort of life as terribly square, even horrible. But what they don't understand is the struggle that lay behind it. On the other hand, the honest, hard-working man, the old-fashioned breadwinner like my dad, had to go a long way to understand the kids."

In season, he would enjoy hunting, taking Bernie with him. They would shoot deer, rabbits, pheasants, quail. But Craig, even at an early age, could not get himself to kill an animal. If he considered it, it was because he wanted to please his father and have more in common with his older brother. It was, for example, his reason for trying to play football, but his heart was not in it.

As with other hobbies, the father's reading was limited in time and scope. The *Reader's Digest*, at times. He watched television occasionally, mostly in the company of his family. He was a man with too much energy to be a spectator. His trips to the movies were few, a matter of some frustration to his wife, who enjoyed them. He was especially firm about not using profanity in the home and, as a precaution, seldom used it outside—even when hunting—a rather extraordinary discipline after over two decades in the armed forces. "To this day," Bernie remarked, "I have never heard my dad say anything vulgar. My uncles respected him so much, they never spoke profanities in his presence. The first time I

ever heard my mother curse, I was around fourteen, I
think, it almost broke my heart, yet all she said was
'damn.' "

For years, Bernard, Sr., was a heavy cigarette smoker
until, as Bernie put it: "Craig and I shamed him into
quitting. Now he smokes a cigar every once in a while,
but that's all. Craig himself never smoked, convinced of
how dangerous it was to health. He was the kind of kid
who got others to stop. He was very firm about that
with girls, for instance. He simply insisted they didn't
smoke when he was with them."

Bernard, Sr., was born and brought up Catholic, but
Dolly Ivins was a Methodist, not highly oriented toward
religion. It was agreed that the children be brought up
as Episcopalians, a compromise of sorts. It became a
family ritual, then, the Sunday morning visit to the old
Saint John's Church in Chew's Landing, and the boys
were trained to believe in its cleansing impact on their
souls. By the time Bernard, Sr., returned from the Air
Force, Bernie, Jr., was an acolyte in the church. Craig
and his father took their communions together. Bernard,
Sr., even became an usher, a vestryman, serving addi-
tionally on the governing board of the church, a duty
that gratified his need for spiritual service. Over the
years, he went to church with some frequency and felt
good when he did. "Uplifted," as he liked to put it. His
wife had considerably less contact with the church,
though she appreciated its impact on her soul. Bernie,
Jr., once remarked: "Mom got to feeling good if she
merely walked in and walked out." The boys, meanwhile,
said their prayers before going to sleep, taught as children to kneel at bedside in the classical manner—"Now
I lay me down to sleep . . ."

Through the early years of their father's absence, the
two boys had grown up no less disciplined and no less
loved. Their grandparents, Jesse and Dolly Ivins, together
with their mother, had no trouble coping with their up-
bringing, and the brothers developed their own life styles
in a properly structured family unit. Craig, musically inclined from an early age, enjoyed an upright piano in
the house which he learned to play by himself. In elementary school, he played saxophone in the band. He

began playing guitar as soon as he got his hands on one. At school, his grades were average, neither excelling nor failing in any subject. Comments of his teachers on old report cards indicated he was not fulfilling what they considered to be his potential: "Not progressing as he should. Lazy." "His school work needs more concentration." "Not trying as hard as he should. Spends too much time talking." "Craig is careless in his writing and spelling." His friends remember him in those pre-teen years as "very likable," "always joking around," "fat and funny."

At home, however, he was more subdued, principally, one assumes, because he was the kid brother. Bernie, in high school, was an important athlete, a big man whom everyone talked about. There was no way in which the stout, unathletic, unscholarly, "lazy" kid could compete with him.

"I guess, as older brother, I used to bait him at times to irritate him. If he had something he thought was important, really important, I would tend to put him down, saying it was nonsense. I guess I even found pleasure in it, a bit sadistic, in a way. Then, too, I could be really loving. Too few shades of gray. When I think back on it, sometimes I think there was a natural repulsion between us—Craig and I, Dad and I, all three of us for each other. Dad didn't recognize it; he didn't see it or understand it. But Craig did, and we learned to cope with it. We discovered that we could rock each other with hostile words and put-downs, really go at each other, but we knew why and we didn't hate each other for it. The only thing was, it was unfair to him. After all, I was four years older and he was a fat little kid.

"Yes, I'd pick on him, but if anyone else did the same, I'd go at him. Nobody else could do that to my brother.

"I suppose a lot of this was because Dad would take me on the same way I took on Craig. I knew he loved me, but he had a way of challenging my manhood so that my feelings would really be hurt. He would call me 'Babe,' for example, and it would embarrass me, especially in front of others. And you couldn't tell him to stop. You couldn't say, 'Please don't call me "Babe" or "Hon." ' He wasn't the type you say that to. He would be

shocked that you would think him guilty of such a thing.
I had done so many things to establish my manhood, I
had really made something of a mark in the community
—only to go home and be treated like a child. It was
humiliating. Craig understood my feelings in this. In the
last few years, Craig and I discussed everything openly.
We would make a joke of it, though he shared my embarrassment whenever it happened. He was extremely
perceptive."

Dolly Badiali was the kind of person who always saw the
best in every situation, no matter how troubled it might be.
A perennial optimist, as it were, demonstrating an endless
faith in human decency. ("You taught me all the good
things in life," Craig had berated her, "and none of the
bad.") It followed that she would hate any disciplinary
confrontations. She was lenient, and covered for the
boys in hopes of avoiding conflict. "If Dad would tell
Craig to be home at eleven, she would pull Craig aside
as he went out and say, well, it would be all right if he
stayed out to twelve, but if he was later, he'd better call.
They were gambling that Dad would be asleep anyway
and wouldn't know. But sometimes, he *wasn't* asleep, and
he would catch Craig coming in late, and Mom couldn't
stand up for him in the face of Dad's anger.

"And Dad could really lay you out. Years ago, I used
to get hit. If I were forty-five minutes late getting home,
he'd really go at me. He was an expert at the old ser-
geant bit, and I guess he felt it was better than hitting
—but sometimes I would rather have been hit, he was
so severe.

"But then, no matter how rough he was, he'd always
be apologetic an hour later. He'd come up to my room
and talk it over, explaining what he thought was necessary to do as a father. He had a passionate love for me,
I knew that. He felt the same toward Craig, though he
had mellowed some over the years. Craig got away with
a lot more than I did—or so I thought—which, I guess,
is a regular older-brother syndrome.

"He was always generous with us, too. About money,
for example. If I had a date and needed some cash, I'd
go to him and ask for it. Then he'd act very stern.
('What? Didn't I just give you five dollars?') He'd give

me the whole story of how money was not to be treated
lightly, then another story on the world's economic system and how it works—and then he'd give me seven dollars, more than I would have asked for, and tell me to
have a good time. He just had to get his licks in first,
that's all.

"I don't think my mother understood the relationship
the three of us had. All that passion, it must have
seemed alien to her. All the hostility, it was always
erupting. And she would suffer, not understanding that
we loved each other too."

When Bernie went away to college in North Carolina,
Craig was fourteen, and suddenly, free of all the debili-
tating comparisons with his more competent brother, he
began to develop a style of his own. For one thing, he
liked girls. He had always felt at home with them, beginning with many childhood hours spent playing with a
neighboring girl—an accident of circumstances since,
simply, there were no little boys around. As a teen-ager,
treating them as equals came naturally to him, and for
their part, girls got to know him as a friend. It followed
that in the hectic boy-girl sex-titillation of adolescence,
Craig became a standout; it was as though he were somehow aloof from all the petty giggling nonsense that sur-
rounds the first years of dating.

It was in this period, moving into ninth grade, that he
began his relationship with Joan. It was also the year
when he discovered dramatics. Both would seriously
affect his life far more drastically than anything that
preceded them.

At fourteen, Joan was just another girl he liked, but
dramatics offered him a whole new sense of himself, and
he threw himself into it. In high school, it was traditional
to hold an interclass competition; Craig's freshman class
put on Edgar Allan Poe's *The Masque of the Red
Death*, and he played Prospero. He was big and stout
and eloquent. There was power in his hamming. Most
of all, he seemed at home on the stage, as natural as his
brother appeared on the football field. He gave to the
audience the feel of his own enjoyment, leading them to
share in it in a way that few adolescents can manage.

As a result, the freshman class won, and Craig went home with a new identity.

In the years that followed, drama became the driving center of his life. In his sophomore year, he played a king in Andersen's *The Ugly Duckling*. He joined a local amateur group, the Blackhorse Players, and at sixteen, played the hero, Jonathan Harker, in *Dracula*. Classmate Gail Hillias, who played the heroine, Lucy, thought that "the role was too straight for him; he couldn't do anything with that sort of character and he was impossibly stiff." In the following year, however, he played the kid brother, Buddy Baker, in *Come Blow Your Horn*, and he was perfect. "He actually became Buddy. You could almost see the change in him, in the way he spoke off the stage, making the same moves he used in the play."

To his credit, however, it was not the acting itself that excited him: it was the entire sense of it. The play was the thing. He hungered to be a part of it all, from building sets to directing, even to writing plays. When they opened up the new Highland Regional High School, he worked hard at developing the dramatics program. In his junior year, he was student director of an extraordinary production of a full-length musical comedy, *So This Is Paris*, a single performance that took over six months to prepare. During the course of it, he starred in his class production of a one-act play, *Final Dress Rehearsal*, in which he played the director of a play about to go on. From the audience, a Highland senior, Charlie Kean commented: "It was a great preview of the way he was going to be as director of *So This Is Paris*." The musical turned out to be a tremendous success, its corny, old-fashioned qualities properly styled to the talents of its performers and the needs of its audience. As Charlie Kean remembered it: "At final curtain, the audience was really cheering like mad, calling out for the director to take a bow. When I turned to find him, he was sitting backstage, so pooped he could hardly move out of his chair. It had been that emotional a thing for him. I thought he'd been tremendous, all during the months of preparations. So many different things to put up with. So many nutty kids and all. Myself, I was scared out of my skull just before we went on. But he had taken the trouble to write me a letter and put it in the pocket of my costume. It was a great letter, really, telling me how much he had gotten out of all the work we had done together, how he had come to know me and appreciate me. It made me feel great. I really did a good job that night, and it was largely because of that letter. I mean, it really moved me. That was the way he was. . . ."

It was, then, primarily through dramatics that Craig could find himself. He used the romantic world of make-believe as a setting in which he could best relate to others. It expanded his personality, his talents, and his dreams; and for the first time in his life, he really felt he belonged somewhere.

No less a consequence of this involvement was the impact of his teachers and colleagues, for it followed that those who pursued theater were intellectually and artistically several cuts above the omnipresent jocks and the shop teachers who coached them. He began to think and read and be aware of ideas. If he was always a sensitive boy, he learned how to channel that sensitivity and express himself. He read serious plays, from Shakespeare to moderns like Tennessee Williams. He read the great writers prescribed in his English courses, and he read them with a keener eye. J. D. Salinger's *Catcher in the Rye* fascinated him, Craig's literary introduction into phoniness, his ultimate enemy. He loved *Catcher,* and largely as a result, he began to put his own thoughts on paper. He wrote stories, poems, diary sketches, long letters. If he was, like Holden Caulfield, sometimes self-pitying and morbid, he was also grappling with his thoughts, unafraid to put them into words. His letters to girls were exactly as he felt, however sentimental and romantic, and the more he wrote, the more freely he expressed himself.

One story, apparently, was outstanding. Written in junior English class under Mrs. Wagner, it told of a boy and his guitar, resting from his bus travels at some roadside Howard Johnson's. He saw a girl sitting there alone and lonely, and he played his guitar for her. She smiled, then took it from him, played it herself, neither of them commenting. And when she finished, he took out a card and handed it to her. It read: "I can't speak." She looked at the card and smiled, then took out a card of her own, and it said exactly the same thing. In the end, they separated, each going his own way. . . .

"It was a beautiful story," said Stanley Pietrowski. "He really made you care. It was like so much of what he wrote. You could always tell it was Craig's if you ended up crying."

This compassion became his strength. At a time when his peers were intent on establishing their manhood with aggressiveness and bombast, Craig leaned the other way. He was able to achieve enough confidence in this direction to be tolerant of others. He could face a difficult situation (as when friends would fight) and probe for a lasting kind of solution. He was never satisfied with halfhearted or less than genuine responses. He wanted everyone to be real and honest, and he discovered that the best way to evoke these qualities in others was to communicate with a sense of love.

It worked well: love came naturally to him.

It followed that there was no way he could have missed the impact of his generation's music. Throughout Craig's life it was there and growing, feeding on the disenchantment of the idealism of youth who had grown up under the shadow of hydrogen bombs. There was, for one thing, a folk-song revival that swept across the country with an astounding power, spreading a message of brotherhood and peace, a direct reaction to the highly industrialized, computerized, war-oriented society of the 1950s and 1960s. Said Pete Seeger: "Communicating in the USA is like trying to talk at a crowded cocktail party . . . but singers can do it." Said Joan Baez: "I went to Harvard and sang to troubled intellectuals with the Bomb on their minds."

Singers sang the old protest songs of the Depression and slavery to kids who had grown up in affluence to face a culture they were beginning to despise. The issues were everywhere, some obvious and readily articulated (racism, conformism, poverty, war), while others, more subtle, festered beneath the surface of their lives, needing a more delicate expression. Through it all, there was an alienation from the generation of their parents that went far beyond the traditions of the generation gap.

Kids wanted a whole new identity in the world they
faced, anything that symbolized a rejection of what they
called a sterile-plastic-antiseptic inhumanity. Gone was
the appeal of the gray flannel suit and neatly barbered
look of the aspiring career man, and with it, the music
of Tin Pan Alley's June-moon-spoon inanities. The new
folk music brought them a message of love and compassion and a feeling of togetherness with everyone, attempting to overcome the spiritual bankruptcy they had been
born into.

> Here's my thesis:
> Peace in the world
> Or the world in pieces.

They wrote of Joan Baez: "The heart of her message
is a kind of soft but unyielding affirmation, a sort of folk-
singing nonviolent resistance, where the related threads
of love and freedom run sweetly, sadly, unforced, without self-pity. . . ."

Bob Dylan wrote "The times they are a-changing . . ."
as well as dozens of poetic songs representing a loving
way of life as an alternative of the hypocrisies of American success, a relentless plea for simplicity that carried
far more power among students than the folly of acade-
micians who were teaching the perpetuation of the status
quo. Indeed, folk songs taught them much about what it
meant to be a human being.

Said Joni Mitchell: "If you are sad, then you should
feel sad. The French are good at that. They show what
they feel and in that way purge themselves of it."

There was something about the singing itself that made
it spread. A kid did not merely spin a record on his
stereo and listen—he sang. The songs were designed for
singing, not just listening. They ran from simple quatrains
to free-form narrative verses, poetically loaded with
strange images and new idioms. They didn't have to
rhyme and the rhythms could vary with the shifting
melodic lines. Kids learned to create their own songs;
anyone could do it, a nation full of young poets and song
writers.

The guitar was at the center of the great revival. The

old instrument of uncertain origin (did it come from the
Oriental family of lutes?) had been popular in Europe
since the Renaissance, especially in Spain—the simple
instrument of the common people, seldom appearing in
the classical music of the aristocrats. American kids took
to the guitar with an extraordinary verve, learning to
strum a few chords in an hour or so, and the folk-song
culture thrived in a great do-it-yourself avalanche of
song.

> Sometimes I feel like nothing,
> Something throwed away.
> Then I get my guitar
> And play the blues all day.
> —Old Blues Song

It became very much a culture, directly integrated
into the new philosophy of the young. Simplicity was
the key. The natural man, yearning to be free of the
complexities and cant of the affluent military-industrial-
academic establishment, assumed the looks and styles
and mores of its opposite.

> What shall it profit a man, a man,
> What shall it profit a man?
> To gain the whole world and to lose his own soul,
> What shall it profit a man?

All this came to Craig and Joan in their tender adoles-
cent years, and as with millions of others, it found a
fertile spirit hungering for the inspiration of its message.
It is indicative of their life styles that they did not enjoy
the work-protest songs that were the very guts of folk-
song history. Craig could not identify with the radical
messages of Depression folk heroes like Woody Guthrie
and Huddy Ledbetter. It was the new wave of young personal and poetic singers that sparked him: Janis Ian,
Peter, Paul and Mary, Leonard Cohen, Joni Mitchell,
Simon and Garfunkel.

> A most peculiar man
> He died last Saturday night

He turned on the gas, and he went to sleep
  with the windows closed, so he'd never wake up . . .
And all the people said, "What a shame that he's dead,
But he was a most peculiar man . . ."

He could relate their message to the anguish of his own
experiences and be inspired by it. Fifty years ago, his
grandfather was stirred by the patriotic fervor of George
M. Cohan, and twenty-five years ago his father sang the
songs of Irving Berlin, both of whose works have more
than merely survived. But the music of the 1960s educated and influenced an entire generation far more than
any other. For Craig, it became another passion that developed through his teens. He became a fine guitar player
himself, but it was the essence of the lyrics that drove
him. "It would be difficult to overestimate the impact
that folk music had on Craig," Bernie suggested. He
played, sang, composed, listened to records, went to sleep
by the FM "underground" radio (WMMR) from
Philadelphia. When performers like Peter, Paul and
Mary came to the Academy of Music, Craig was there
in person. He knew every song they wrote and played.
Indeed, he played them all himself. He attacked any
new album release the way an epicure approached a
good meal, little by little, letting his taste buds caress
each new lyric, playing and replaying until every deli-
cious bit was thoroughly savored.

"I guess it began a few years ago when I brought
home a seven-dollar guitar I'd picked up at college,"
Bernie recalled. "Craig learned to play it in no time at
all."

His father saw how much this was his son's direction,
and though it was not especially to his liking he did not
discourage it. In fact, for his sixteenth birthday, he
bought Craig a fine twelve-string guitar. Bernie estimated
that at least forty hours of Craig's week were spent with
folk music, in one way or another—either listening or
playing or composing, and dominating evenings with
friends.

Bernard Badiali, Sr., read the *Reader's Digest* while
Craig was singing Simon and Garfunkel's ". . . the words
of the prophets are written on the subway walls. . . ."

4

"Joan was such a pretty girl, it was sometimes hard to believe she was part of the Fox family," neighbors would say. There were other points of difference that would turn out to be far more significant.

The Foxes had moved out from Philadelphia when Joan was only three, a large family with two older boys and four girls. The twelve-thousand-dollar house was new and brightly situated on a neat little plot a few short blocks from the center of Blackwood. It was a rewarding possession for the hard-working parents. Andrew Fox was a World War II veteran and a truck mechanic who had lived in the city all his life. As with others of his generation, the thriving postwar economy brought him a higher level of financial security than working people were accustomed to enjoying, and he demonstrated his appreciation for this phenomenon with an ardent love of country and the system that made it function. Indeed, the Vietnam embroilment had involved his older son, Andrew, Jr., a few years back, and currently his younger boy, Raymond—both of whom were objects of his pride—necessary sacrifices to perpetuate the blessings of the affluence that was America.

"He's a very nice man," said Joan's neighbor, Gail Hillias. "He was always pleasant when we'd be over there, though he didn't say much. All the kids used to go sledding down the hill at the end of the road near Joan's house. When we finished, we'd go to her house for hot chocolate and cookies, and he'd smile at us, you know, like someone who was happy we were there."

To Joan's attractiveness, she added a vivacity that made her appealing to boys. Apparently, she was sensitive to this at an early age and thoroughly enjoyed the attention she found she could get. According to Gail, "When Joan was just a little kid in elementary school, she would like to stand on the corner, real cute and daring, and she would try to get boys to stop and talk to her, to buy her a soda or whatever. She was always a little boy crazy."

She began dating somewhat prematurely, even by Blackwood standards. "She didn't like to stay home at all," added Debbie Gliick. "She had so many boys chasing after her, there was never any problem about going out."

Joan met Craig in elementary school, then again in Sunday school at the Episcopal Church in Chew's Landing, and they began going together early in high school. Though their dating was not exclusive, they seemed like a permanent twosome right from those early years. "They would have little quarrels all the time," remembered Chrissy Henderson, a perennial classmate of both, "over the usual things, like where they would go on Saturday night, or some disagreement over something they had read. Then, one or the other would make a point of dating someone else, just to get even or make the other jealous, and they would fight some more. But they would always get back together again, just like everyone knew they would."

Joan found something in Craig that captivated her, some rare capacity in a young boy that nourished her need to be a better person. Other boys simply chased after her, doting on her prettiness. If this was pleasing to her vanity, she found little in these relationships to inspire her. Craig, on the other hand, treated her more like a friend who cared. He didn't put on airs to impress her. Nor did he fawn on her. Quite the contrary: he challenged her. In a way, he was even cool to her at times, as though he cared little if she liked him or not. And this, it followed, drew her to him more than ever.

"She was hooked on him, that's all there was to it," Gail said. "Sometimes I used to think she was possessed by him in some strange way. She was so young, but she loved him. She really loved him."

At fifteen, Joan was, by all appearances, a perfectly normal, straight, lovely American girl. She had been brought up in a reasonably structured home, taught the classic middle-class virtues of devotion to God, love of country, respect for authority. She resisted none of these. In fact, she was honestly faithful to them all. In school, she was popular and active; as a result, she was voted to celebrated offices that marked her rising status. Class treasurer, for example, and she was nearly elected president of the student council. She was conventionally ambitious, seeking whatever prestigious positions she could achieve for herself. She was a good student, though not exceptional, and was faithful to the discipline of class assignments and projects. She was a fair athlete and enjoyed the competition of games. If she was too slight for basketball, she was good enough to make the girls' hockey team. She was better than average in tennis. Because the varsity cheerleader squad was, perhaps, the most sought after activity in school, Joan tried diligently to win a place among them—finally doing so at the end of her junior year.

In all these ways, she was loved and admired by her parents. There was, however, little time and energy for them to go much beyond that, what with five other contentious siblings to deal with. Joan, it would seem, had to be the least of their concern: older brothers were going to war, older sisters preparing for marriage.

To Joan, however, life was not the simple matter as circumscribed by her family, school, and community. Her father sat before the television set watching a ball game, and Joan was exploring Henry David Thoreau. It is one of the contradictions of much American secondary school education that though the intent is to open young minds to new ideas the practice is somewhat less inspiring. In spite of all such limitations, however, there are kids who are sparked by a need to explore beyond the classroom. They will take note of Sinclair Lewis's *Main Street* in sophomore English, but they will want to go beyond it—through *Babbitt* and *It Can't Happen Here*, for example. This was teen-age Joan Fox, fascinated by the genius of Lewis exposing the same hypocrisies that appeared in her own background. It was the same with *Catcher in the Rye*. She read voraciously: Hemingway, Walt Whitman, early John Steinbeck, the ironic James Thurber.

She would relate what she read to the essence of her

own life and, inevitably, it began to create confusions and troublesome questions. Go to school and learn, say the parents. Read Thoreau, say the teachers. The young mind struggles to understand and adjust, suddenly seeing that neither parent nor teacher understands the impact of such a treasure. In fact, the nature of their lives indicates exactly the opposite: conformity, submissiveness, materialism. The old adage gets reversed: Do as I *do*, not as I teach. Joan was torn by this clash of values. She was blessed with beauty and a desire to exploit it, because this was what she was trained to do. If other girls, less popular, less appealing, envied her, if they constantly engaged in petty competitive pursuits, and if they were insensitive to others and eventually destructive to themselves, they were all nonetheless friends because that was the way things were, that was the way a normal girl was supposed to get along. She began to see herself as one of them—as, indeed, she was—and she did not like the image.

And always, there was Craig. "She always wondered what he thought—about everything," Gail said. "She had her own opinion and, many times, she would argue with him. But you could see that they were growing up together, no matter how often they fought."

It was true; their relationship was a stimulating one, for both were going through constant changes. New values, new interpretations kept upsetting the old. Yet they also tended to cling to what was rooted in their backgrounds, maintaining security within these limitations. Although their minds were exploring and questioning, they were cautious, not rebellious. They wrote poems and songs and they violated no rules.

At sixteen, Joan found herself increasingly drawn to Craig, an emotional dependence unlike anything she had ever felt for anyone before. She could not picture herself ever being without him. "They were like two peas in a pod," said a friend, Bob Brower. Almost reluctantly, she would go out with others, like Dennis Stewart, good-looking athletic classmate, a pleasant, straight boy who was always there for her. In fact, when she did quarrel with Craig, he would tell her to go out with other boys, that they shouldn't be tied together. "No

rings, no strings," Craig would say. So she would give
him back his ring, or his pin, and they would break up.
She would toss her hair and go out with Dennis, but she
would suffer through the separation far more than Craig.
In just such a period, in the summer of 1968, she wrote
her friend Ginny Kamulda a letter revealing her despair.
"I get so afraid I'm going to lose him, I don't know what
I'm ever going to do. . . ." Ginny said: "Joan went out
with other boys, but she would never talk about them.
It was as if they didn't really exist. It was only Craig she
cared about."

Her life was active, for the most part joyous and
spirited. Along with Craig, she threw herself into the
excitement of dramatics and enjoyed them immensely.
She joined the Blackhorse Players as well as the school
productions. She played guitar and sang folk songs and
wrote poetry. Ginny remembers how she met Joan at a
folk-singing fest at nearby Berlin City Park, three summers back. "We were singing a song called 'Rider' in
those days. Joan really liked that song. Then there was
'Today,' 'Bamboo,' 'Autumn's May,' 'Changes.' She was so
beautiful and when she sang, her face would really light
up, she made everything come alive. . . . It was because
she knew how to express her true feelings. She used to
say that too many girls were like blank walls, they never
opened up what was going on inside them."

Indicative of (and contributing to) Joan's changing
values was her growing relationship with Desi Worland.
In Blackwood, Desi was truly an anomaly. Born in Ore-
gon, deserted by her parents, raised in a foster home,
raped and impregnated at fourteen by a foster father,
crisscrossing America to South Jersey, she ended up with
a hard-drinking foster mother in a battered home on the
outskirts of town. At sixteen, Desi was bright and talented (in music and art), deeply troubled, and, above
all, determined to survive. If she thought of herself as
fragile, actually she was closer to being indestructible.
She was an appealing girl, her large made-up eyes
twinkling and challenging, constantly amused and amus-
ing, always quick to react from a wellspring of both love
and rage. She was a passionate child, laughing and crying, ready to stand up to an abuse, an injustice, an in-

humanity. Yet she was subtle, too, and worldly-wise, having learned from the grotesque chain of experience that was her life, and she was prepared to learn more.

For over a year, she was very much in the center of Joan's life. "When Highland High School opened, I was the school hippie. Hardly anyone would talk to me. They'd all heard about my background, how I was supposed to be all screwed up and all, and what with the way I dressed and looked, I guess I was something they were supposed to avoid. Then, one day, I went over to a fountain in the hall to get a drink, and Craig pushed the button down for me. I looked up and he was smiling and he said, 'Hi.' Nobody had ever done that to me before. Then, when Stanley came to Highland—he was the second hippie—we mimeographed some sheets to organize a Be-In at Berlin Park. Craig and Joan came. I'd lost my guitar there and Craig said he thought he saw some kids with it over by a tree, and he went over and got it for me. Then he showed me his classical twelve-string and we started playing together. That's how we became friends. He and Joan went out of their way to befriend people. They really liked everyone. I mean everyone. I remember one time, this kid I knew with a crazy way-out rock group in Philly, he was all strung out with problems, he was in bad shape, people wouldn't listen to him, wouldn't talk to him. I mentioned it to Joan, and she got very upset and said she would try to help him. I gave him her phone number to call, and they would talk for hours. She really helped to get his head straightened out. She was wonderful to him, and she'd never even met him."

Desi, for all her vitality, had comparable needs, and she found in Joan the kind of simple, honest friendship she had lacked all her life. She was not overwhelmed by their differences any more than Joan was.

To Joan, Desi was pure fascination. She admired the purity of her rebelliousness. Joan was like a baby chick trying to bust out of its shell, and Desi was there for the hatching. "Joan would tell me how foolish she felt being what she was. Sometimes, she hated it. Like being a cheerleader because it was the thing to do, because it was supposed to have status, because she thought that, somehow, Craig liked the idea—but then it turned out that he found it sort of silly too. She was like two different people, the way everything was pulling her one way, then the other. She used to think she had to put on an act to be accepted. She thought she had to do prestige things even though she didn't really enjoy doing them. That's what everybody told her to do so she did them. One of the reasons was, she wasn't very happy at home, there was so much hassling going on between all her brothers and sisters. She was such a gentle girl, so lovely, it must have upset her terribly, but she would hardly ever talk about it. She didn't want to gripe. She wanted to find the positive things."

With Desi, Joan would open her mind and be understood. She could examine her motives and put them in perspective. Desi was a challenge to her identity and Joan knew how much she needed that.

"One day last spring [1969], we went to Philly together, just to get away. It was a beautiful day and we walked along the river. I was feeling playful, but Joan wanted to talk. She was searching for a purpose in life, you know, like maybe you had to leave something behind to make your life worthwhile. She was so serious, it moved me to rap with her, not that I had any answers. She was trying so hard to make sense out of life. I remember, she'd tied her hair back instead of letting it down to her shoulders—it was such a waste, she was so pretty, I kept pulling it down. I just wanted her to enjoy what she was.

"We went down to the Square and some old man tried to pick us up. You know, he sees a couple of hippie-looking chicks and he wants to get in on the free-love kick. Joan was so embarrassed. Then, there was a long-haired kid who came over and offered us some dope. Joan really got upset. I told her that he was only trying to be friendly, really. But she said that was like somebody offering you a little lung cancer. That was Joan, so straight. She was really hung up on the straight thing. And sex . . . she was guilty about sex . . . very middle-class. It really frightened her. It was the same with the status business. She could never really free herself from that status business. Once, in school, we were talking to-

gether in the hall, and a few of those cheerleader kids
came over to her. She knew they didn't like me, so she
just walked away with them. Just like that. She wanted to
be identified with them and not with me, and I guess she
thought it was important that she do what they wanted.
She called me up that night to apologize and I really
yelled at her. She was so ashamed. She said she didn't
know if she could ever pull herself together. I told her
not to worry about that, she was so lovely, you just had
to understand her."

They would call each other almost every night and
have long, serious talks. "She was changing and she
wanted to talk about everything. I guess she needed
someone besides Craig to open up to. I know I needed
her just as badly."

Then, almost without warning, Desi ran away from
home.

"Everything seemed so wrong for me in Blackwood.
I was sick of being a foster child in a home where everything choked me. School was dreadful. I wasn't learning
a thing. I would try to find excitement with friends in
Philly but my foster mother decided that she didn't
like them and tried to cut me off from them—just because they had long hair. So, one day, I put on my
floppy hat, took my guitar and a few things in my bag,
and went to Philly. . . ."

No stranger to the big city, she teamed up with a
group of sympathic, equally troubled kids, and plunged
spiritedly into communal life.

It stunned Joan. "She came to Philly to see me; she
brought me food and books *(Leaves of Grass, Main
Street)* and a few things I needed. What fascinated and
frightened her was the boy-girl thing, living together like
that. She was very middle class about morals and all, and
the thought of me sleeping in the same room with boys
was too much for her. She was so shy. She felt she
wouldn't be accepted by my friends, that everyone would
think she was a terrible prude. Then one of the boys
tried to make a joke of it and called her 'Superstraight,'
and she just about died."

For all of Joan's scruples and inhibitions, Desi's impact
was a potent one, eventually enabling her to cross the

line into a higher level of liberation. Joan would explore these shifting values with Craig, and in time, sensed a greater freedom to think and act and feel than the restrictions of their backgrounds had encouraged. It was in the spring that they finally consummated their years of inhibited sex play.

It followed that their relationship would achieve a new plateau, though at first they were frightened by its power over them.

"It was a silly business for them to get so hung up about," Desi said. "If they couldn't understand that there was nothing wrong with sex, especially since they loved each other, they would just have to learn to grow up with the problem."

Desi, meanwhile, was having serious problems of her own. Her group had become involved with marijuana and were under a continual surveillance by the "Narcs." Desi said: "I just knew that sooner or later we were going to get busted. It happened in June. I was charged with 'Conspiracy to procure and sell,' with bail set at one thousand dollars, and there was no way that I could get up that kind of bread. There was no trial, just a hearing. The court put me down for legal aid, but they didn't get it for me. No lawyer from the moment I was arrested to the moment I finally left prison, three months later. I never so much as spoke with a lawyer."

She had left the dehumanizing dullness of her life in Blackwood for the ultimate corrosiveness of prison. She was permitted no phone calls. All make-up and clothes were stripped from her. She was given an old sack-dress and torn sneakers, and deposited in a row of cells in company with the beaten-down dregs of Philadelphia's ghettos. "It made everything seem so hopeless. You can die in jail and no one would care. The weeks roll by and you keep thinking that this will be your trial day, but it never comes and you can't do a thing about it. Everyone says you'll get out soon, that they can't hold you like this without a trial, but you keep sitting there, waiting."

Joan was horrified at the plight of her friend, especially since she was not permitted visiting privileges by the prison authorities: no minors allowed. She wrote, only to discover that mail was censored and sometimes not even delivered: "I think of you often and I can hardly bear the thought of you there. I know it must be a terrible place, but don't let it destroy your sensitivity. Please!" Craig wrote her, too, and both tried to send her things. Nothing was permitted. Desi could not even have a guitar. "They said it would have made me a privileged character. I guess that prison was the only truly democratic institution in America," Desi quipped. "A guitar would have made me so happy, it really hurt. What burned me up was that the men had instruments, several of them. But I didn't have any money. You needed money for everything. If I had any money, I wouldn't even be in prison, I guess. I used to draw portraits for two cigarettes each. 'Don't let it destroy your sensitivity . . .' I really cherished Joan's letter. I thought how so much of my life seemed to doom me to this sort of place, and how completely the opposite was Joan, yet she had all this love for me. Then I'd wonder what her parents would be saying about me. . . ."

It wasn't until July that they finally summoned Desi for trial, but even then, no lawyer was available. The judge was about to send her back to jail, CFN, Continued until Further Notice, but "I broke down crying in court, I couldn't go back, I thought I'd die if I went back. The judge finally said, okay, he would let me go because my foster mother was there. I could go if I lived with her again, and I would have to stay until I was eighteen because I was a ward of the state.

"When I got home, Joan and I talked for hours. I told her everything. She insisted on that. She wanted to feel what I had gone through, and I wanted to tell. I think I wanted to try to shock her with the truth, about how awful it was and how I wasn't going to take shit from anyone any more. She was so sweet, she cried. She said she thought I had become a little harder, but she didn't mind. She said she understood, and that she didn't think she could have gotten through it all. Then she said she wished she could be more like me, and that made *me* cry."

5

Whichever way Craig turned he confronted the uneasiness of his growing pains. He kept looking for a way to reach out and grab something new. Though he enjoyed the intensity of his love for dramatics, he was not content to live within its protective cocoon. He constantly tried to expand his interests and experiences. His life seemed to be too tightly circumscribed by the crunch of local pettiness. He saw the turmoil in the world, and though he knew little about its causes, he was ashamed of his lack of involvement. Too many kids did not seem to care—poverty, race problems, war, all these indications of inhumanity were distant from their lives. It pained him.

There was, however, one boy in school who was much the opposite, and Craig admired his activist stands. It seemed that Ed Bonnet was always in the center of current problems. For the 1969 elections, for example, he organized a vigorous local campaign for the eighteen-year-old vote in New Jersey (LUV—Let Us Vote). He enjoyed politics and studied its techniques the way a fledgling attorney would hang around courtrooms. He was one of ten children in a Catholic family, his father an official in the United States Immigration Service. The background was conservative and patriotic, and Ed understood the value of such an orientation, especially in the local adult community where the power lay.

In the fall of 1968, Ed was leader of a local group known as Students for a Free Society, and organized a march to Camden in support of American Soldiers in Vietnam. Craig and Joan joined in that march—it seemed to them less like a war statement than a simple statement of concern. Above all, it was a commitment and Craig wanted to do something. If he was naïve about the over-all significance of the march, at least he could show that he cared. The more politically sophisticated Stanley Pietrowski tried to talk him out of it. "He didn't know what he was doing then. He was joining the local prowar gang. I was counterdemonstrating that march, and Craig was very upset. He just didn't understand politics at the time. He really thought that being against the war was unpatriotic. Of course, that changed. Later he became ashamed of going on that march."

Craig was slow to develop an antiwar position, for home and school, the structured centers of his existence, both demanded an outspoken support of the Vietnam war. Dissenting opinions had to fight their way through chinks in the wall. Stanley helped begin his education, readily assisted by Desi, then followed by Liz Quemore. All of them agreed, however, that Craig would have changed without them. Said Stanley: "He was not the type to stay put. When I first came to Highland, he was nice but terribly straight, but you knew it was just a matter of time before he cut loose." Stanley, like Desi, was bright, artistic, rebellious, but did not share her capacity for a deep relationship. He liked Craig but was more amused by many of his attitudes than tolerant of them. Still, they held many opinions in common, a basis from which their friendship could grow. "For one thing, we both hated gym. What a waste of time. We couldn't understand kids getting upset over losing some silly game. They'd be on the verge of crying, some of them. Wow, we could never understand how that could be. . . ." Then, too, they enjoyed the same folk music and went to Philly for that first Peter, Paul and Mary concert at the Academy of Music. "Craig really got flipped out by 'The Great Mandala.' When he got hold of that album, he would play it over and over." It was a significant choice, for the song dealt with a boy who was jailed for his opposition to war and starved himself to death rather than conform.

Craig was undoubtedly envious of Stanley's independence, his capacity to defy his parents and take long weekends in Philly or New York. Stanley seemed more like a big-city character who had been displaced in Blackwood rather than reared there. "When my friends would come out from Philly to visit, the kids around here thought of them as real weirdos. The big haircuts and wild clothes. Like once I was dragged down to Mr. Keegan's office at school because I was seen by a teacher splitting my candy bar with a friend. They suspected I was passing dope! They called in a detective from the Gloucester Police Force to question me; I guess it was just too big for the school to handle. The way they thought of me, if the principal, Mrs. Forneron, had gotten syphilis, they would've blamed me.

"What struck Craig and Joan as exciting was that they found they really had a lot of the same ideas as we did. The trouble with them was they just couldn't free themselves, even though they hated the way they were. Like Craig—he would come to think in a hip way, but he was always careful not to rock a shaky boat. That's the trouble when you come from a solid home. He loved his parents too much. His father was nice but tough. A typical old army man. I guess he didn't like me, and the way he was, I can't blame him for that. When I went over there, he would sound off in favor of the Vietnam war and how we had to destroy communism. Craig would take off to his room, leaving me to fend for myself and be slaughtered while he would be playing guitar or listening to a record. Mrs. Badiali was very nice and I always thought she understood a lot more than she would say."

In junior English class under Mrs. Wagner, Stanley's opinions and contributions were not suppressed. "I'd get up and read poems by Ferlinghetti, for instance. There was nothing like that in our English texts. Allen Ginsberg, too. Craig really flipped over them, and he borrowed my poetry books, even copied some of his favorites. When he wrote his own poems, there was no doubt but that Ferlinghetti influenced his style. He liked that free kind of expression. . . ." It was much the same with Stanley's taste in theater. He believed that Craig was all hung up with the old-fashioned plays they put on in school, like *Cheaper by the Dozen* and *The Mouse That Roared*. Stanley took him to Philadelphia to the avant-garde groups at the Theatre of the Living Arts and sub-

jected him to the dramatic anger of their generation,
another telling blow toward liberation.

"Then there were these terrific coffeehouses I hung out
in, like The Trauma. Craig got to know them and love
them, and we'd sit around and play music and talk.
When I'd get that hemmed-in feeling, I would take off
sometimes to Philly just to get a breath of that smoky
room."

It was at the core of Craig's problem, this conflict of
identity and loyalty. He tried to keep his two worlds
apart and disliked himself for doing so. "What is straight
and what is hip, and what exactly was he? That bugged
him. He wanted to be able to communicate with everybody, and it bugged him that he couldn't. The more he
understood about himself and life, the harder it became
for him. He used to tell me how it was important that
we do something for the rest of the kids in school, to get
them to feel deeply and communicate with each other,
but they were just a bunch of lunks, most of them. I
told him that he would have to accept the fact that they
weren't worth the trouble, that he shouldn't be bothered
with them. But he couldn't think that way. He *had* to
care. He *had* to try."

To many of Craig's old straight friends, Stanley was
something of an intruding freak whom they did not care
to understand. But then, Craig was Craig, unlike anyone
else they knew. Suffice to know that he liked them too,
and they shared his friendship as always. They were fine,
bright, talented, responsible—they represented the essence of what their community expected of them—and
would do their best to live up to such expectations. Bill
Billhardt, Jr., Craig's colleague in dramatics, co-producer
of the musical *So This Is Paris* that had consumed so
many months of their junior year, found warmth and
understanding in his friendship with Craig. Bob Brower,
older and less cerebral, shared his companionship on
double dates and trips to the shore, and enjoyed "lots of
good times together, just joking around and all." Young
Mark Bunzell was exceptionally personable, ambitious,
very much in earnest, and found in Craig a sympathetic
"older brother." "I think he liked the idea because he
was a younger brother himself. He would take me to

Philly to show me around, the places to go. I'd never really seen Philly before, except once or twice with my parents to go to a store, maybe. He was always welcome in my home and I always felt the same in his." They all saw him daily, and noted the changes in him but were not disturbed, for there remained that solid, deeply compassionate part of him they could always relate to.

Bruce Conway, though he had never been a special friend of Craig's, was nonetheless affected by contact with him. "There was one guy in school, we'd been in the same classes for a long time, and he was always coming up with those weird puns and jokes that would get you annoyed. You'd get so you couldn't take him at all. But Craig, he said if you thought about it, you had to hand it to the guy because he had the guts to be himself. He was trying to be funny. And so he was an original person, unlike others, and that if we didn't know him so well, we'd be more tolerant of him. Well, I thought about it, and when I faced that guy again, I really didn't mind him so much.

"That was the way Craig was. He saw the nice things about people, and he could get you to do the same."

His special friendship during his junior year was with Frank DiGenova, part of a remarkable family of young scholars. Frank was quiet and conservative and admired by all. A year ahead of Craig, he represented the highest level of achievement at Highland. To Frank, "Craig was remarkable for his ability to make you feel alive and needed. He genuinely cared about you, especially if you felt you were in trouble—and I guess I usually was." In effect, Craig had found a perfect friend for himself: someone who was respected by all for the best reasons, and needed him. Frank's problems were Craig's meat. For one thing, Frank was in love with classmate Ann Schramm, a lovely, bright, sensitive girl with an eager curiosity and an unsettling hunger for involvements. It was, however, a shaky relationship for him; he was not at all certain he could rely on it when he needed it most. For another, he was torn by his own multiple talents—to be an engineer at Rensselaer Polytechnic Institute or a humanities student at a liberal arts college. And beyond these definable problems were the myriad others, the self-doubts, the anxiety over one's purpose, the quest for meaning. Frank could spill them out and Craig would drink them in; and they would wrestle with their mutual bewilderment over the nature of their lives in a way that made living seem far more palatable. Among sensitive teen-agers, depression is not an uncommon affliction. ("Happy teen-agers can be terrifying," a psychiatrist once noted. Or, to paraphrase the German playwright, Bertolt Brecht: "The kid is laughing because no one has told him the bad news.") Frank, apparently, had discovered the "bad news" and was doing his fair share of suffering, the roots of which lay classically in the boy-meets-identity crisis. The higher the expectancy ratio, the greater the crisis. The greater the sensitivity, the more difficult the solution.

Craig was there for him, finding the hidden key that could open the door to another day. "It was a very valuable friendship for me."

Then, in the spring of 1969, Craig discovered Liz Quemore, resident niece of the maverick Quemores of the converted red barn, a large, freewheeling family headed by a jazz musician with Indian blood (they called him "Chief") and his wife, Betty, an ex-teacher turned social worker. The Quemores were the most liberal and outspoken family in Blackwood, their door always open to anyone seeking friendship, their kids deeply involved in sports, art, music; many of their activities as straight as any of their peers, yet totally alive to the changing youth culture and its growing rebellion against war and concomitant evils. Lizbett was another artistic girl, extremely pretty, petite, with long dark hair. Craig got to know her creating the sets for *So This Is Paris* and a relationship began. When Craig reached one of those periods of estrangement from Joan, it ripened into something more. It was a strange combination of diverse background and orientation, of straight and hip, of tall and short; they were, in effect, opposites in many ways, yet each of them felt a need to identify with what the other represented. Craig approached Liz with trepidation. Though he had known many girls, he had never been romantically close to anyone like her. To add to his anxiety, he discovered that she liked him, a fact that both gratified and intimidated him. Said Liz:

"I had never been with anyone that straight. Like the way he dressed, for instance. Just those plain chinos, a shirt, a pull-over sweater, always neat and all. He would tower over me with that big square face and horn-rimmed glasses, his hair short and barbered and combed. He would call me at night and we'd talk, and then once, I told him I had to get off the phone and that I'd call him back in a few minutes, only to discover he was talking from a phone booth. He didn't want his father to hear what he said, especially about the war in Vietnam. He wanted to talk about that because it confused him. I used to think he actually supported the war just to keep peace in his home. He loved his father—he had grown up close to family—but this business of the war was getting to him. He would challenge me to argue with him. Of course, I would. I would talk about the political side of it, but that got me nowhere. When I asked him if he could go over there and kill another human being, he saw what I meant, and that stopped him. He began to agree with me after that.

"He also wanted to talk about pot. I would try to explain to him about the satisfactions of smoking communal style, how you express yourself openly when you do, how everything comes out freely. He didn't want to do that, though. When he finally got some pot from Desi, he would turn on by himself.

"One night, we went out, double-dating with Frank and Ann. We drove out to Lakeland Hospital and parked by the pond. It was very peaceful. We played guitar and sang. We bought ice cream—cherry vanilla. I remembered the flavor because Craig wouldn't let me smoke, so that taste remained in my mouth for a long time. Then we settled in the back of Frank's station wagon, lying there close together. He kissed me, very gently. I'd never been kissed like that before. Then he pulled away and I knew he wanted to talk. But he couldn't. He didn't know what to do, so he began to caress me, to touch my body. It was odd, but it didn't seem right, so I asked him why he was doing it. He stopped, but he didn't answer me, and we just lay there quietly while he looked at me in the dim light. It embarrassed me. He must have seen that, too, because he got up and excused himself. While he was gone, the police drove up, poking around the wagon, looking for pot, I suppose, but all we had was ice cream. They asked me if I was eighteen because it was late and unless you're in a moving car, you have to be home for curfew. We explained that we were waiting for Craig and that we'd leave as soon as he came back. But he didn't come back. We waited a long time, and finally the police came back, annoyed this time, because one of them had stepped in a soggy ice cream container and gotten his shoes messy. We had to leave, finally. Craig never did come back with us. He called the next day, Saturday, to apologize. He told me he just wanted to go off by himself, an urge he had to gratify. He'd caught a bus home.

"It was a strange night, but when I thought about it, it didn't seem strange for Craig. He could do things like that and he was so genuine, so real, so honest about his moods, it seemed perfectly natural for him.

"He wrote me a poem on Saturday:

> Remember Hemingway
>   Said 'Courage' is most
>   Important
> But remember, also, he
> Put a bullet through his head.
>
> Frank said 'Effort' is
>   Most important
> Perhaps the chances
>   Of his becoming a
>   beggar are not that slim.
>
> Pencils have erasers because
>   People are people
>   But what bothers me is
> !! my pencil always outlives
>   my eraser!!

"I read that poem a dozen or so times that day and wondered about him. It was strange; later I came to think it was the other way around with him: his eraser was outliving his pencil.

"On Sunday, he took me to the shore with him. We went wading in the surf and he gave me a tiny little shell and asked me to keep it forever, but when he lifted me on his back for a piggyback ride, I accidentally dropped it. I was very sensitive about that, but he laughed it off and gave me another and kissed me. Later, his mood changed. We were sitting on the dunes and he put sand in my hair. I got angry about that and deliberately smoked a cigarette in front of him.

"The whole thing ended soon after that. It just sort of drifted away, though I did like him a lot. Even though he was so different—or maybe because of it. He was so nice, so kind, so understanding. But he lacked strength. He wasn't hung up about it, he just didn't have enough courage. He would look for a way to avoid following something through. Joan was like that, too. She was a cookie-baker. She would bury herself in the kitchen with her sugar and flour and all. Once, when they were split, she made some cookies to please Craig, but she asked me to give them to him. I thought that was rather sad. . . .

"Still, I liked him and he liked me. I guess the thing with Joan was too much to overcome. I could almost tell when he would be thinking about her, like that night at Lakeland when he left the car. . . ."

Liz Quemore, like all young girls, has a small box in which she keeps a few treasured possessions. Among them, there are that poem and a tiny shell. . . .

It was as if part of Craig were trying to break away from Joan, trying to find some new identity to establish his independence. He wanted to grow and he wanted to do it alone. He was feeling the constriction of his life in Blackwood, an endless cycle of preparation for nothing, of going nowhere, of being hemmed in by uninspired minds and his own incapacity to rise above them. He was almost seventeen years old and there wasn't any light showing at the end of the long tunnel. He loved his parents and, because of it, was all the more frustrated by their inability to share in his groping, to help him answer those endlessly tormenting questions.

His brother's return from college in late spring was rewarding, despite the inconvenience of being forced out of his room. Bernie, Jr., his wife and baby with him, pumped new life into his sagging spirits.

"He had changed a lot," Bernie noted. "Even his body had matured, finally losing the young fat he had been carrying. He was big and husky, but not overweight. Well over six feet tall, maybe one hundred eighty pounds. But all the action was in his head, and he couldn't wait to get it out."

Craig found an understanding ear, especially since his brother's views were comparable to his. In addition, his sister-in-law, Margie, was equally responsive. The presence of these two was a valuable trade for his room.

"One thing became clear to me about Craig," Bernie noted. "He needed time away from home. In college, I had met a marvelous old couple in church—the Reeveses —they were seventy-nine years old. They had a lovely place in the hills outside of Brevard and they invited me to visit. I really loved them. When Mr. Reeves died during my sophomore year, I offered to stay with her, knowing how she must be suffering, needing the help of a man. I received permission to live off campus, and I stayed in her guest house, chopped wood for her, did a lot of chores. I loved it, enjoyed being alone, out of the noisy dorms and all, and I'd read by the fireplace and study with a sense of peace I'd never known before.

"Well, then I thought, wouldn't it be great for Craig to live there for the summer? He had spent a week visiting me and he'd hit it off fine with Mrs. Reeves. Besides, there would be plenty of action for him, what with the Brevard Music Fair. After all, it was a resort area.

"Craig enjoyed the prospect of going. He could picture himself walking those hills, thinking, reading, writing . . . the whole idea of being alone in that setting was like offering a starving man a job in a bakery. But it just didn't work out, perhaps because my dad thought he was too young to spend a summer that way. He was just seventeen on May 24 (the same date as Bob Dylan), and instead, Dad gave Craig a car."

"I think Craig suffered with the whole idea," Frank DiGenova commented. "He knew his father loved him and wanted to make him happy. He liked having the car, but he let it become sort of a symbol to him, a car for not going, even though he knew this was not the case. I sympathized with him, but I also thought how tough it must be to be a parent."

"The car was part of a three-way swap with uncles and cousins," Bernie remembered. "A truck for a Chevy for about one hundred dollars in cash for the car. Dad would try to convince us all that he had gotten the best of the deal. It was all sort of a joke, of course. . . ." It was a light blue 1962 Falcon sedan.

6

The end of school is the beginning of summer, a time of release and holiday, of new pleasures and responsibilities, of parting and anticipation. Its sentimentality is always reflected in the annual ritual of inscriptions in the school yearbook (it is called *The Heather* at Highland) and Craig's was lush with them.

> Craig: I figure that there isn't much that I can say that can equal what you wrote me in your letter without sounding like a weirdo. So I'll just say that I never met anybody who was so nice and understanding. I wish you all the luck in the world that should be yours. Respectfully yours, Charlie Kean.

> To someone I hold very special now, and I hope I always will. Please stay my friend, I need friends like you. Stay as you are, Craig, this world needs more like you. I'm not too good at writing in yearbooks but I put what I feel. Deb. (Remember me, please.)

> I don't know what any of this means but at least it's clean and uncensored. Love and peace. Stan.

> Craig . . . It saddens me to write this, as it saddens me to see the sun go down. I wish it didn't have to be. But then, everybody wishes. If you ever think of me, don't picture me as a scientist, politician, happy, lonely, or anything. We tried to help each other once. Take that. And if you won't treasure it, at least save it and maybe one day it can mean very much. Frank.

Don't try to fool us with your clothes; we all know
you're hip.

Craig, it's been quite a year. Mrs. Diane Wagner.

Love and beauty, rightest and best
My thoughts seek you as
Waves seek the shore
And when I think of you I am at rest

Remember me always as a parasite in your life
Sharing many of your joys and sorrows, walking
parallel to your steps of experiencing many adventures.
See you next year when we add to our album of
treasure. Gail.

In the front of the book, there was a published paragraph or two for the seniors from Joseph Moffa, president of the Board of Education in Gloucester Township:

. . . A great many events have occurred during your
high school years that have changed the course of
history. You have experienced some historical events
that have hailed the hallmark of our times. The
success of Apollo Eight is one of these happenings.
This should inspire you as graduates to forge ahead
to make this the greatest nation in the world.

I say stand up for what is right and just for all
mankind. Do not be influenced by the militant forces
that are out to break down the sphere of law and
order that has served our nation so well for generation upon generation. Do not let these moments of
violence take root in your lifetime. . . .

There was no note, no poetry, no inscription in Craig's
book from Joan. They did not wish to liken their relationship to any other.

As summer began, they were together again; it was
as though it had never been any other way.

Summer is vacation from school, but work is always an essential part of it. From preadolescent years, it was traditional for Blackwoodians to find ways to make their own pocket money—mowing lawns, paper routes, delivery boys, caddying, berry-picking, etc.—ways familiar enough to preceding generations when a teen-ager had to learn the value of money.

Since the South Jersey shore was less than an hour away, much of the summer action took place on the beach and its environs. Parents would frequently take their two-week vacations in and around Atlantic City. Everyone knew someone who had a place at the shore. Many kids rented apartments together and took jobs at the resorts to sustain them. Others would drop down for a few days.

Bernie, who was an expert swimmer and senior lifesaver, worked at a private lake a few miles from their home, while Craig got a job at the nearby Haddonfield Music Fair, where a series of summer productions needed the help of eager young apprentices. It was an ideal setup for him, another experience in the world of theater and music, especially since Joan found work there with him. They built sets (she also worked on costumes), assisted in lighting and design, ran errands for such stars as Martha Raye, Mickey Rooney, Gary Puckett. It was all very glamorous and big league, and they looked forward to the drama of each new week. In the end, however, it depressed them, for the world of show business thrives on rootlessness and artifice. People were seldom what they seemed or honest in what they said. Emotions were erratic. To Craig, it could be summed up in his reactions to such trivia as the way Gary Puckett would come on stage with leather jacket, boots, bell-bottoms, etc., reflecting his image as a rock singer, only to take off his costume at the end of his recital and dress in a double-breasted jacket, wing-tipped shoes, neatly combed hair: the straight costume of his proverbial enemies. Joan, in turn, was far too socially oriented to settle for this; hungering to make a contribution to someone, somewhere, she found herself assisting her friend Debbie Gliick in a summer program for young kids at the

Methodist Church in Blackwood. Craig, meanwhile, began seriously considering the Peace Corps as a future commitment to his ideals, which Joan was happy to share with him.

Meanwhile, on days off from the Haddonfield Tent, Craig submitted to an old yearning to see New York City. Inspired by his friend Stanley (who told him how it was easy to hitchhike to the city but difficult to get out of it), he plotted a trip with a friend, Bill Jones, deceiving his parents as to his plans in order to stay out overnight (since New York was definitely off limits), and off they went, eighty-five miles up the Jersey Turnpike. In New York, they had very little money and no one to contact, so they walked, from Central Park and the Bethesda Fountain to Greenwich Village and the phantasmagoria of its nightly street life. Craig later told friends that for the first time in his life he saw identifiable homosexuals and hippies who dressed zanier than he had ever imagined. They fed on hot dogs and soda from street peddlers and retreated to the Port Authority Bus Terminal to sleep on its benches. Craig met a girl named Cecil with a bizarre hairdo and struck up a friendship that would continue in correspondence. It was a trip he enjoyed, for the city fascinated him. He had found those special areas where young people congregated as if they owned them, pockets of a giant city seemingly populated exclusively by kids, meeting like friends in a great fraternity independent of parents and other adults. They wore beards and uninhibited haircuts and marvelously elaborate clothes, and their buttons spoke of peace in the world with a passion and unanimity that staggered him.

However, he felt alien to this scene for it went beyond his capacity to absorb. It was, as he put it, just too much. Yet, needing another taste of it, he returned several weeks later, trying to picture himself in such an ambiance, but there was nothing in his experience to permit it and, in the end, he went home sensitive to his limited capacity to belong. (You can take the boy out of Blackwood, but . . .)

Craig was changing, to be sure. He was feeling the pull of America outside the confines of his home community.

He was reading more, exploring more, intent on learning more. Like a lost kid asking directions, he would question others, probing into their minds that he might expand his knowledge.

He was persistently perplexed by the problem of style. If hair was the manifest symbol of the youth rebellion, he could readily see how too many of its devotees were along purely for the show and not for the truth of it. Craig's response was inevitably defensive for he was unwilling to be lost in a jumble of categories that were marked by appearance. His young friend Mark Bunzell was sometimes amused by Craig's reaction to the problem: "He always used to swear that he would never be seen dead in a pair of bell-bottoms, but one day we were going to the shore, and there he was, wearing a pair of bell-bottoms." Bernie had the explanation for that: "I had bought a pair, but they were too big for me around the waist, so I offered them to Craig. He tried them on, just for laughs, and they fit him perfectly. So, just for laughs, he said he thought he'd wear them one Saturday." It was as much of a departure from his own uniform as he would ever make. "I don't think Craig would ever let his hair grow. Not that he objected to others. It just wasn't his way."

It was a long summer for Craig, and he took to spending idle hours in his room, reading and writing. He filled several notebooks with poems and reflections on his growing confusion and resulting sadness. He was seventeen and just becoming conscious of how little he really knew. As a result, he was challenged by everything he confronted. Fortunately, there was someone special, right in his own home, with whom he could rap.

Margaret Trocolli Badiali, his sister-in-law, was a beautiful young mother with a remarkable serenity for one her age. Warm and sympathetic, she was an ideal recipient of his constant need to expose his ideas, especially since there were no strings attached and no history to complicate his emotions. Besides, he liked women. He liked to talk to them, especially this built-in gem of a woman with time on her hands and compassion in her heart. What's more, she didn't just listen, she challenged him. ("You are always moaning about the lies people tell, but you lied to your parents when you went to New York; you told them you were going to Atlantic City.") He appreciated that kind of talk, and it liberated him from many of his own restraints, knowing he would always get honesty in return for honesty.

Between his brother and Margie, he could explore things more fully, and everything became fair game: movies, politics, religion, sex, people. "He reacted to everything as if it were about himself," said Margie. "He was the kind of person who wanted everyone to be happy but couldn't be himself. If he had a million dollars, he'd be all the more tortured by the poverty of others and he'd give it all away and then he'd be unhappy because it would have barely made a dent."

Inevitably, there would be talk about the Vietnam war, especially since Bernie had come home from two years in college with a passionate antiwar orientation. "Craig was eager to be convinced that the war was a mistake. The whole notion of our burning and bombing was horrifying to him, but like most people around Blackwood, it was even more horrifying to think that the United States could be unjustly involved. We talked about that and he came to see how it was possible. He was not a very political person, but he felt so deeply about killing, it offended him, forcing him into an antiwar stand. Then, too, he began to see that poverty and racism and pollution all sprang from the same political system."

He would read articles in *Time* and *Harper's,* and developed a growing sense of the hypocrisy of his country's posture. "When I saw him after I got out of jail," Desi Worland noted, "he was all hopped up about it. He was carrying around a page from a magazine* that told how everything we were doing in Vietnam was the opposite of what we were being told. We rapped about that for a while, about how we were all trained to think a certain way, the so-called patriotic way, and this was how the whole system kept going, that it kept on getting worse and worse but nobody was able to do much about it. That really upset him. America was supposed to be the greatest country in the world, but there were all these evils and the government wasn't doing anything about them and nobody seemed to care."

Harper's Magazine, June 1969. John Kenneth Galbraith's article, "How to Control the Military."

7

If the most joyful day of the school year is the last day of the spring session, the runner-up is probably the day of return in September. By mid-August, the days become shorter and the night air begins to chill, bringing on an anticipation of rejoining friends unseen for many weeks. Who went where over the summer? What happened? What new styles, new relationships, even new thoughts, would be forthcoming?

For teen-agers, high school is the structured center of their lives, guiding them through adolescence with an awesome power to dominate their life styles if only because it brings them all together. It has been said of the American secondary school system that its primary—if unstated—purposes are to serve as a continued baby-sitter to keep overstimulated youngsters out of trouble, and to hold them out of the competitive job market for a few more years.

"Highland High School," said a teacher who requested anonymity, "is the perfect reflection of the community." Indeed, there are very few complaints about its educational limitations. If school discipline is rigid and relentless, it is no different from what the student is accustomed to in his home. Blackwood parents, it could be categorically stated, are not prone to permissiveness.

There was a depressing starkness about the school's appearance that reflected its essence. Its masonry, for example, did not lend itself to wall hangings, and the long corridors made of building blocks stretched cleanly from end to end. "The only pleasant-looking room in school is the library," said the teacher. "It has books against the walls."

There were other, more basic deficiencies in structure:

"I worked on the original construction," noted young Charlie Kean. "I could tell that the footing was not going to be set deeply enough. We were slopping around in the mud, and the next thing I knew, they were pouring the cement foundations. It didn't make sense. It wasn't but a year later that the walls began to crack, real big slashes, some of them. And the gym floor, after that first winter, it had lumps in it; it really began to buckle."

One might also say that even as the building was completed, the entire plant had become obsolete: classrooms were overcrowded by opening day and there was talk of split sessions in the offing.

If there was pride in the spanking new complex of buildings and athletic fields in the autumn of 1967, it began to dwindle with the cracking walls. Its very newness seemed to breed a spate of restrictions that severely limited the free flow of ideas of teachers and students. The school administration became increasingly centered less around the educator than the disciplinarian. "The best way to the top of the Gloucester Township school system is to be a phys ed man," commented a retired teacher. "The best way to the top of the school board is to coach a Little League team to the championship," said another.

The neatly painted walls remained bare and clean. There were strict rules about smoking, chewing gum, tardiness, gathering in halls, excessive time in toilets; a demerit system was instituted that frequently resulted in suspension.

As for studies, the range of subjects taught was adequate, but the emphasis was clearly nonacademic. There were twice as many gym teachers as social studies teachers, as many shop teachers as English teachers. Significantly, of twenty-one hours of history scheduled each week, nineteen were devoted to the United States and two to the rest of the world. The curriculum was divided into vocational and academic programs, with a far greater percentage of the former. Boys were trained to work at trades, while girls prepared for nursing and homemaking.

"You can't teach democracy in a totalitarian setting," someone wrote on a classroom blackboard. It was one thing to create a disciplined structure in a school; it was another to maintain it with reason and respect. Typical of the student resentment against too much regimentation was the crisis in late September 1968, barely a year after the opening of Highland.

The issue was trivial, yet grating. The administration policy was to allow five minutes between classes, and tardiness was marked with a demerit, eight demerits leading to suspension. Suspension was punished by three days' confinement in a special room, prison-like, windows high above eye level. The suspended student was required to sit at a desk for the entire school day, neither talking nor turning in his seat, continually monitored by a rotation of teachers not otherwise assigned. Students hated that room, hated the kind of discipline that put them there. There were even a few cases of kids who flipped out, unable to cope with its claustrophobic impact. There had been a number of complaints from responsible students about this, especially the five-minute rule that created so many demerits; in the sprawling complex of buildings, classrooms might be too far apart and halls too crowded to negotiate the distances in the prescribed time. Even the Student Council had brought the matter to the administration, all to no avail.

The events of that mild September morning were a phenomenon inexplicable even to those who so eagerly participated in them, for there were no leaders, no planning, no organization. It simply happened. A number of kids arrived early on that Wednesday morning, nothing unusual in itself. They hung around the parking lot, ostensibly waiting for the eight o'clock bell that would admit them to the school building. The talk was all about the five-minute rule and the severity of discipline; somehow, no one knew how or why, everyone gathered to join in—a crowd attracting a larger crowd. When the bell rang, suddenly, again without plan, dozens of kids began to honk their horns. "It was like the sound of trumpets!" said Charlie Kean. When a few turned to go inside, others shouted at them to stop. They became several hundred strong, and very much aware of a rising sense of power. By eight-thirty, well over half the student body remained in the parking area, various kids taking turns to speak out for the unity of their protest. The assistant principal, Mr. Keegan, came out, as did a number of teachers, alternating pleas and threats to break up the rebellious demonstration. It was not without humor that football coach John Konstantinas—tough, crew-cut, authoritarian—told them all that he would send the varsity football team to force everyone inside physically, only to be greeted by jeers and uproarious laughter, for most of the football team was participating in the protest.

Board President Joseph Moffa appeared shortly after nine (most of the students had never seen him before and didn't know who he was) and asked them all to go to classes, promising that the administration would meet to settle their demands. "Nothing can be done until we have a reasonable atmosphere in which to meet," he said. It was reported in the Blackwood *Observer* on the following day that Moffa had seen to it that all students were back in classes by ten-thirty. According to others, however, hundreds were still out there until after lunch hour.

"The teachers came out and were very threatening, especially to seniors," Liz Quemore said. "They said they would prevent kids from graduating if need be, that they'd put this on the school records to make it difficult to get jobs, that they'd get them thrown off teams and other extracurricular activities. They did scare a lot of kids back inside."

"Actually, it was a beautiful thing," said Stanley Pietrowski. "You could see how it frightened the administration."

According to the *Observer*, the students became sufficiently organized so that they refused to return to classes unless the administration would promise that there would be no reprisals. "We are students in the greatest nation on earth and the most free, and we demand to be treated as such," ran the student declaration of purpose. "We oppose an unjust demerit system, as though we were not capable of distinguishing right from wrong."

In the end, they won a compromise victory on lengthening time between classes from five to eight minutes— and little else. In Charlie Kean—who chanced to be interviewed by a CBS radio reporter, Herb Rambeau from Philadelphia—the school adminstration had what it called "the ringleader." Said Charlie: "I was given three days of the very suspension system we were protesting against."

If the adminstration was indeed frightened, it had no real reason to be. This was not a student body responsive to any organized committees even vaguely prone to a rebellious stand. In fact, had there actually been such an organization attempting to plan and provoke the demonstration, the entire scene never would have happened at all. The kids would have run from it as if it were the plague itself. As it quickly became evident, the administration was not in the least intimidated, certainly not after school returned to normal. Its modest readjustments to disciplinary procedures allowed the protesters a token glimpse of victory, but only a token. Above all, it was made vigorously clear that no such action would be tolerated again, and all those participating would suffer appropriate punishment.

"They made us feel ashamed," said Chan Quemore. "If they'd put us on bread and water and beat us with rulers, you couldn't have gotten another protest going."

"The students are like sheep and Mr. Keegan is the sheepdog," said Stanley. "Mrs. Forneron [the principal] is the shepherd and she takes orders from Mr. Moffa, who runs the whole damn pasture."

"Sometimes I feel sorry for Mr. Keegan," said Desi Worland. "I'd like to drop some acid [LSD] in his morning coffee and watch him blow his mind. He's so caught up in *de*merits, he never sees any merits."

"It's the system," Stanley added. "Like once there was a hassle in the cafeteria and the teacher reported that I was throwing food. They brought me to Mr. Keegan, where I rapped for twenty minutes on my own moral code about how I don't waste food, that it's a crime to waste food. I told him everything I believed about that, but he just sat there and didn't say a word. Then, when I finished, he said, 'But the teacher saw you do it!' I got four demerits, because that's the way the system works. He's trained not to believe the student. It's a crime to believe the student."

The cafeteria was, apparently, repeatedly an arena in the controversy. Ed Bonnet recalled a time when he was carrying his loaded tray to a table when a teacher abruptly bumped into him and food was spilled. It was an accident for which the teacher was responsible, but Ed found himself being berated for his carelessness. Offended, he asked that the teacher apologize, an action that aroused the teacher's anger and brought Ed before Mr. Keegan on charges of insubordination. "I wasn't going to let them beat me on this, as trivial as it was, I didn't want to let them get away with it. I knew one of the cafeteria workers and she had seen exactly what happened. I finally got her to testify for me, a dangerous thing for her to do, taking a student's side against a teacher." In the end, the charges were dropped, but Ed was not done with it: he began campaigning for a student-administration tribunal wherein disciplinary action could be reviewed by an impartial board.

To the great majority, however, Highland Regional High School was their alma mater and, knowing no other, it gratified their educational and social needs. Even the bright students were not without pride in the nature of its functioning. "The school is okay," said Bill Billhardt, Jr., Craig's highly responsible friend. "I don't want to say anything against the school. If you do what you're supposed to do, you don't have to get into any trouble with anyone."

That was it in a nutshell. Compliance was the answer, especially for those with limited goals. There were several adequate teachers and, if the cards fell right for you, there was enough room to spread one's wings in various directions. Even those with artistic inclinations could find a sympathetic teacher to work with, and if the school board was dangerously receptive to pressure from the nonesthetic groups who did not want their tax dollars wasted on such effete programs as painting and sculpture, somehow these activities managed to survive. The discipline and restrictions were part of life, and only the more sensitive and sophisticated found it insulting. Said Gail Hillias: "The administration always seems to expect the worst in the kids. You can be telling the truth, but they never believe you. They always assume

you're lying." Liz Quemore, fumbling with her developing political awareness, found other frustrations when she
sought an airing for her expanding views: "I'd get involved in a political discussion in class, about poverty,
say, or the plight of the blacks in ghetto areas, and sometimes, if I were arguing well, I'd think, well, maybe I
was going to score some points this time, maybe I was
making a dent in someone's head. Then someone always
says, but that's 'radical,' or 'that's communism,' and
immediately, everybody rejects everything I've said. I
mean, it's crazy. It's impossible to argue; no one will
listen. It doesn't matter how true or real or how right
you may be, if someone cries 'red' you're dead. And the
teachers . . . wow . . . once I tried to prove my point
in spite of this, and the teacher said: 'Let's face it, Lizbett, you *are* a bit of a radical, you know.'

While students across much of America were showing
an ever-increasing need to protest, their demonstrations
were an anathema to the people of Blackwood, the September protest at Highland notwithstanding. The students
at the high school understood that and accepted it. Nonetheless, it galled them to be treated with a demeaning
view of their maturity and intelligence; indeed, many of
the rules imposed upon them were actually self-defeat-
ing as disciplinary forces. If they were asked to rush
purely because rushing was supposed to keep them out
of trouble; if they were punished quickly, without adequate examination, thereby sometimes victimizing the innocent, it was done because all punishment has a preven-
tive impact. If the administration was secretive wherever
possible to keep underlings on their toes; if everything
that was oppressive and sometimes unfair was done under
the guise of being best for everyone, authority exists
solely for that purpose and must not be questioned
without sacrificing the welfare of all. All this, too, was
what one was supposed to put up with. They were not
trained to protest, but only to comply. They did not
question, they did not challenge, and, above all, they did
not defy. And those few who dared to do so were looked
upon as freaks.

Said August Muller, Superintendent of Schools: ". . .
Everybody in this world has a burden. This in itself is

relatively unimportant. What is important is *how you carry it*. My challenge to you is to carry your burden well."

"Beautiful!" quipped Desi Worland. "Somewhere, before the Civil War, a Georgia plantation owner must have said something like that to his slaves."

By the autumn of 1969, however, there were students who would tell you that perhaps seventy per cent of Highland High School's thirteen hundred students had discovered that their burdens were possibly too heavy; to lighten them, they were sampling a substance known as marijuana.

It was perhaps the best known secret in the history of Blackwood. Indeed, if the august Mr. Muller was aware of this phenomenon, he made no mention of it. Nor did Mr. Moffa of the Board of Education, Mrs. Forneron, the principal, or even Mr. Keegan himself. Since ordinary smoking was not permitted in school, how could the school contend with the far more serious problem resulting from this flagrant violation of Federal law? "The truth was, more kids were smoking pot than regular cigarettes," said Desi. "It was like outlawing kissing but ending up with an epidemic of VD."

To the kids, it was all something of a lark, no more serious or illegal or defiant than a Saturday night beer party out on Bloody Bucket Road a few miles outside of town—and a lot easier to conceal. The stuff was no problem to obtain (Camden was fifteen minutes away, Philadelphia just across the bridge); it seemed no more unconventional than looking at pictures of nude women in *Playboy* magazine. They were normal American adolescents and they were eager to experiment. Most of them had tried whisky, and pot was not damaging to their stomachs. Though many did not go beyond the sampling stage to satisfy their curiosity, to others it became a choice pastime; they were indifferent to the dangers of exposure. "Turning on" in Blackwood became as normal as driving a car.

"Blackwood," said Stanley, "had finally become part of modern America."

Through it all, however, a stranger could meander within the halls of Highland Regional High School (if he

managed to get permission), sit in its mannered classrooms, observe the neat and orderly students, and see
nothing that would be alarming. (It is indicative of their
compliance with conventional Blackwood morality that
a straw poll in 1968 showed sixty-three per cent of the
students *opposed* the legalization of marijuana. The
school functioned with that same formidable control built
into its unsullied concrete walls, and except for a relatively few and minor incidents, the educational process
moved steadily and surely toward its limited goals.

Nor were there racial problems of any consequence.
As with the population ratio in the community, blacks
constituted a very small percentage of the student body
—no more than twenty-five out of the total thirteen
hundred. Except for an argument or two, there was
peaceful compatibility—though not without tension.
(E.g.: Chan Quemore had lovely long blond hair, and
when one black student admired it, even wondered how
it might feel to his touch, she laughed and told him to
go ahead and touch it. He did, and when several white
boys saw this, they wanted to beat him up.) It was not
without relevance that, in that same 1968 straw poll,
the most popular political figure vying for the presidency
was George Wallace:

Wallace	38.26	per cent
Nixon	34.27	
Humphrey	15.79	
Others	12.68	

One teacher remarked: "When Highland gets as many
as one hundred black students, I shudder at the prospects."

There are other teachers who will point with pride at
its special achievements—as when a nationwide campaign
was conducted to raise money in support of the 1968
U.S. Olympic team, and Highland's contribution was the
largest recorded throughout the entire country. On another occasion, the student assembly welcomed a general
from the Pentagon who spoke of the need for all young
people to back the soldiers in Vietnam with some per-

sonal token of their support. Immediately, the student body decided to run a competition among home rooms to see which could amass the greatest contribution. The kids brought in books, phonograph records, games, clothes, even money. "It was the most fantastic thing you could think of," said Stanley. "The government was spending billions on the war and some public-relations general gets us competing to send CARE packages." Liz Quemore said: "It was terrible, you couldn't put it down. It would be like spitting on the flag if you disapproved. Why weren't we asked to give anything to the suffering kids in Vietnam?"

The school was proud of this kind of achievement. If the varsity football team did not fulfill the hopes of its athletic department, the wrestling team became consistent champions of the South Jersey conference. And the marching band, led by the diligent, ambitious bandmaster, Joseph DeMenna, became known as one of the outstanding bands in the entire state. "The band, the band . . ." complained Charlie Kean, a fine rock musician himself, "everything stopped for the band. When the Artisans [the dramatic society] spent practically the entire year putting on the musical [*So This Is Paris*], we sold tickets and filled the auditorium, but the proceeds didn't go to improve the dramatics program, it went to the band!" DeMenna took the band all over the area, playing concerts and marching in competitions to great successes and rising prestige.

Highland's faculty was excellently varied with young and old, men and women. An overwhelming majority were alumni of Glassboro State College, beginning with basic salaries of six thousand dollars, with increases of three hundred dollars a year to a maximum of twelve thousand dollars. Two were black, teaching nonacademic subjects. Most were career men and women, wanting to rise in the system and advance themselves accordingly. "It is," as one ventured to suggest, "a tightly run ship," precluding any open acknowledgment of deficiencies, its crew having long since learned that "disloyalty" was punishable by harassment and eventual discharge. Typically, Mrs. Diane Wagner, one of the most popular teachers on the staff, was disinclined to be critical of school policies even after she had left the Gloucester Township school system, though she admitted the existence of "some very unfortunate things that went on."

As one teacher commented: "Highland High School is like an antiseptic hospital where all the patients seem well cared for, but no one ever recovers."

All was not static, however. In the infectious culture of teen-agers, styles and patterns are constantly in flux, each year more rapidly than the last. On opening day of school, September 1969, there were, for example, many apparent changes in the looks of the student body. "It was mostly the new kids, the freshmen," Stanley Pietrowski, a senior, was quick to note. "They were like a new breed. They came in with a different look, not all of them, of course, but enough to make you sit up and take notice. Longer hair, for one thing. And the girls, they looked much older than those kids were supposed to look. But mostly, it was the way they talked, like they knew all about what the scene was. They were thirteen years old and they couldn't wait to climb off the school bus so they could light up a cigarette, and you knew they were ready for something more."

"They didn't seem at all like freshmen," said Liz Quemore. "It made you wonder what had been happening in the elementary schools."

Said the seasoned, embattled ex-con Desi Worland: "It made me laugh, the way they dressed, for instance. They'd seen that look on some dumb teen-age TV show out of Hollywood and they thought how daring it would be. Their mothers probably went out and bought it for them. You could bet, one sour word from Mr. Keegan, and it would all be changed. This was Highland High, not Berkeley."

The look was new, but, as Desi had indicated, an extra inch of hair on a boy did not constitute a rebellion or even a change in thought. It had all too frequently been said: "Nothing ever changes in Blackwood; it just becomes more so."

For the seniors, it was the beginning of the last lap in the long run. The best and brightest of them would presumably go to college, delaying marriage and the draft in the process. Most of the others were resigned to their fate. It was significant, however, that though their fate was statistically predictable, very few of them were prepared to make any predictions.

Craig and Joan were among the dubious. His directions were amorphous, though he assumed that he would end up in college. It did not escape him that he did not fit into any of the easily prescribed patterns. There was nothing in the future he could see himself doing, no specific professional goal that sparked him. Certainly, there was nothing related to his studies in this final year in school. He was fascinated by the theater, but he was nonetheless aware of his limitations. Yes, he could go to college, at Glassboro, perhaps, where his brother was now going, and study dramatics. For what end? To teach? To become an actor and try his luck on the professional stage? Was that what he wanted? He had no other special talents or inclinations, no drive to law, or medicine, or science—none of these had ever interested him. For one thing, he had never been enough of a student. He had seen his brilliant friend Frank DiGenova orient himself with a dedication that was awesome, straight A's that led all the way to Rensselaer Polytechnic Institute. Craig envied it and was confused by it, for he was not inspired to those standard goals they were all supposed to work toward, the security and affluence and respectability that goes with making a success of yourself. He saw it all around him, a whole community of security-minded adults, and kids very much like their parents. What annoyed Craig was not the money they had, but their total involvement with its pursuit, and always at the sacrifice of any meaningful involvement with other people.

This, of course, was at the root of his interest in joining the Peace Corps. He could reject the call to affluence and, at the same time, not be rebellious; for he could not see himself as a rebel, only as a participant in working for the welfare of others. A do-gooder, yes. He would nurse a sick bird back to health, and therein communicate a message of humanity. If it was only a trifle, even if no one else was aware of it, it was a symbol of what he believed to be right in man. The Peace Corps was a way to find the best expression of his self and, perhaps above all, to get free of his roots. Significantly, except for Joan, there would be no other volunteers from Blackwood.

This isolation of his values only added to his distress. He was having enough trouble finding his identity and desperately needed the approval of his own generation. But his peers, created in the image of their parents, pursued the predictable cycle, justified principally on the ground that the son would improve his lot beyond the scope of the father—the progress of America from generation to generation. As Bernie described it: "Blackwood kids don't want to leave. They see no purpose in trying to make a different kind of life for themselves elsewhere. They settle for a routine job, buy a home and raise a family, get a new car every year or so, and stay with the same friends they've known all their lives. It's the safest formula known to man."

Craig's friends were aware of his confusions and commented extensively on the change in him. "He seemed so much more serious than he used to be," said Debbie Gliick. "He used to kid around a lot, say funny things and really laugh, but he did much less of that in the fall."

"He cared about everything and everyone a lot more," Mark Bunzell said. "He would be distant at times. The thing that was the same was his niceness."

"He came back to school a troubled boy," noted English teacher Diane Wagner. "He was looking hard for answers. He always wanted to be with those who asked the questions."

"He was troubled, all right," said Stanley. "He began to see that this country was a mess and that he couldn't ignore it. Not any more."

"When I went away to school, he gave me a peace medal," said Frank DiGenova. "He said I was supposed to wear it and think about it, and then pass it on so somebody else could think about it."

"He talked about the war a lot," Desi said. "Like he hated the business about body count, killing reduced to a contest. He said the war was brutalizing America."

It was a time when Craig and Joan became inseparable, their need for each other had become so great. Craig reached out for her like a man who finally knew what he wanted. And Joan curled under his wing, content to do whatever she could to please him. "She was beginning to lose her self, her identity," said Debbie. "She told me of a love scene when they were baby-sitting; she was lying with her head in his lap, looking up at him, and he said to her that he was thinking such deep, loving thoughts about her, it was more beautiful than anything he had ever felt before. And Joan, she was so moved by it, she wanted to cry." Then, typically, when Craig received demerits for cutting gym and was suspended, a few days later, Joan got herself caught smoking and was suspended too, just to share the suspension room with him.

On the surface, however, their lives during those early autumn months went very much the way they had always gone. Joan was now a varsity cheerleader and was exhilarated by it, yet Chan Quemore, fellow cheerleader, could elaborate on the ambivalence of their reactions. "It was something you did and enjoyed but you knew it was wrong for you. You were doing it for the wrong reasons, really. It was fun, the excitement of the football games and all the people, but deep down what you liked was that all the girls envied you and the boys thought you were special. It was a status thing. For a girl, being a cheerleader was about as prominent as you could get. That was the silly thing, and it led to cliquishness. Joan and I stuck together pretty much and tried to have as much fun as possible, but the others could get pretty stuffy. Like the business with the uniforms. The school uniforms weren't fancy enough for them. One of the girls came up with the idea of adding to it: a new jacket, another kind of flashy hat, and others decided, sure, it would be great, even though it would cost us each sixty-three dollars. I got my mother to try to stop this. Joan did too, and the two mothers sent letters to the school in protest. But the eight others wanted to do it. Some of the parents could hardly afford the extra money, but you could bet they'd scrub floors to get their kids this extra stuff, just to keep up with the Joneses and all. Nobody dropped out. Nobody."

Cheerleaders. Color Guard. Majorettes. Marching Band. Football. It was the essence of teen-age America on sunny autumn Saturdays. Let the whimsical Desi Worland describe her reactions: "They'd haul us out of school about two o'clock on Friday afternoons and everybody had to take a seat in the bleachers for the weekly pep rally—apparently more important than anything that might have taken place in the classroom. I would sit with my two or three long-haired friends and we'd make fun of it all. Craig used to sit with us and we'd wave at Joan and keep waving until she'd wave back. The band would come out and we'd sing 'The Star-Spangled Banner,' then they'd parade. I'd clap for them, I liked a lot of kids in the band. The football team would run a few plays, pass, kick, call signals, and all that, and the coach would make a speech about how great the team was; Mr. Keegan would too, telling us how they were going to win the next day. From what I heard, though, they seldom did. But everybody would cheer and while they did, we'd be singing 'Up against the wall, Mr. Keegan!' They had to break us up after a few weeks of that."

Craig, meanwhile, was president of the Artisans, and together with Mrs. Wagner, began planning a production of *The Mouse That Roared*. They would meet in Mrs. Wagner's home room at three o'clock, ostensibly to discuss the play and its production needs, but in time, these gatherings branched out into nontheatrical subjects. A daily bull session, as it were. Stanley, Desi, Craig, Joan, two or three others with varying consistency. It was a friendly place to meet and talk, and there was no limitation on discussion. "We used to shock Mrs. Wagner," Stanley said. "We'd open up about masturbation and sex and all. She was a very proper lady, very nice, but sort of cold and unemotional, it seemed. Like the image of a fashion model. We talked about the war once or twice, but it never got off the ground. I think it was because Mrs. Wagner would turn off when it came to the war. I don't know if she favored it, but she certainly wasn't against it. It never seemed right to discuss the war with someone like that. It was almost embarrassing."

Stanley had been attending group therapy sessions at the University of Pennsylvania, one of which took him to a large room, painted all white, and (as he described it to them) "for four hours, you were in there and did whatever you wanted. You ran around and screamed or climbed the walls, whatever.

"Craig and Joan, they said, Wow, let's start right now and get a group going! They really thought it would be something great. Joan said she wanted to get herself in a scrunched-up position and just sit there and let her mind go wherever it wanted. And Craig, he wanted to have a big window he could look out of, a window that opened on a lot of people and things going on. He wanted to look out on people. . . ."

Needless to say, it was a project that never got off the ground.

"Mrs. Wagner was nice, and she always tried to be helpful," said Desi. "Craig and Joan liked her a lot— especially Craig—but she wasn't enough for them, she really didn't understand them. Like she thought that the real Joan, deep down inside, wanted to be a beauty queen, all made-up and all, Miss May Day, or whatever. But Joan never wore make-up, not only because Craig didn't like it; she just didn't believe in it. Joan had really changed in the last year and I guess Mrs. Wagner didn't really believe it. Joan had even stopped wearing a bra, shocking the girls in gym class. 'What, you're not wearing a bra . . . !' "

There was more levity with other friends, as one warm Saturday evening in September, when Craig and Joan were with Mark Bunzell and decided to do something light and silly. They picked up Debbie Gliick, rousing her out of an early sleep, stopped off at the 7-11 to buy hot dogs and a box of marshmallows for roasting. They drove out to Bloody Bucket Road with its dark uninhabited surrounding woodlands and a vague history of nefarious doings (it was rumored that the Mafia used to bury its victims there). Their fears, however, were less about spooks than about police, for it was traditional that the police would patrol these roads on Saturday nights looking for pot smokers, drinkers, or trespassers. No matter what the activity, there was danger of arrest, even if it was only a wienie roast. "It's a little thing, but there it is, and it hangs over your head no matter how straight you are," said Mark. "There's no crime problem in Blackwood, but there's no freedom to act like you want to. Some people say that's why; the cops prevent crime by scaring you into behaving. . . ."

(Stanley, for one, put a different interpretation on it: "It's all designed to suppress kids, and it does more to create problems than to control them. It stifles kids . . . like at the senior class beer party a year ago, way out on Bloody Bucket Road. The cops came. Their party hats spinning, everybody threw away their beer cans; nobody got caught violating that great New Jersey law against drinking under the age of twenty-one, but they got busted for creating a public nuisance on the roadside. You aren't even allowed to use a deserted part of nowhere. There just isn't any place to go. Like at the Burger Chef [a hamburger stand on the Black Horse Pike]: you're not allowed to hang around the parking lot and meet friends; the cops come and force you to leave, no loitering, no loitering.")

On this particular Saturday night, to the four kids, this anxiety over the police was merely an addition to their trumped-up sense of adventure, and they enriched their moods with a collection of eerie stories. Said Mark: "We finally settled in a quiet spot, found some wood and got a fire going, then sat around playing guitars and singing. Debbie was frightened, though; she kept saying she heard strange voices, and we kept kidding her with more ghost stories. Then, suddenly, we actually did begin to hear what sounded like a primitive drumbeat, a stick on a large pail, maybe, and it got closer and closer until, just as suddenly, it stopped. Dead silence. And that was even more scary. We sat there huddled together, and Joan was laughing at Debbie, but you could tell she wasn't particularly amused. Then, wow, from out of the woods came the wildest scream I'd ever heard. We jumped like rabbits—nobody ever moved as fast as we did, and we threw everything into the car and cut out of there, laughing like crazy but scared out of our skulls. We ended up on Bee's Lane, and sat around talking, laughing about the whole business. Craig told stories about warlocks in South Jersey he'd heard from his grandfather who'd lived here forever, and when we finally drove home, we were singing crazy songs and joking and laughing so wildly it must have been like being on acid."

It was the kind of silly adventure Craig and Joan were straight enough to enjoy. "Most of the kids around here are always trying to convince each other how sophisticated they are," said Debbie. "They smoke pot and drink and talk big—it's such a dull thing to watch them pose away the hours. With Craig and Joan, you could really be yourself. You could have a nutty night like that and be honest with your feelings. I really felt that I had one of the best times in my life that night."

It was during this period, however, that Craig and Joan began to spend an increasing amount of time apart from their friends. Some took note of their withdrawal. Desi, for one, berated Joan: "I told her she seemed to be going into a shell, that we hardly ever saw her except in school. She apologized, saying she felt like being alone with Craig, that she had no other needs. We would talk on the phone at night, but it wasn't the same. She really seemed distant at times."

"Craig was content to stay in his room alone a lot," Bernie noted. "It wasn't typical of him, yet it really wasn't strange, either. He was sort of Byronesque, a big romantic fellow, like that night in Frank's station wagon out by Lakeland Hospital when he left them all wondering about him. I could see where he might enjoy doing that sort of thing, knowing he would leave a reaction. I remember once, I dated a girl in high school, a cheerleader, and she didn't like the way the evening was going, and she said: 'Let me out of this car!' So I let her out, right there on the highway, and she had to walk home. She told the kids about it in school—as I knew she would; it was something people talked about: 'What? You let her out, in the road, at night?' One couldn't help but enjoy that sort of talk."

Craig lingered in his room and wrote poems, stories, sketches. His product was extensively subjective and his mood consistently depressed.

> You wonder how a man could look
>   at the face of another
>   and kill him.
> You'd think the horror would be
>   too great.

You'd think a man would have to tear
    his soul apart.
One night I dreamed of war.
Real, it was.
    Terribly real and sickening.
I dreamed of a helicopter
    hovering over the jungle
    like a hawk circling to find his prey.
There was a soldier
    perched at the open door
    resting his weary arm
    on a machine gun
    cigarette hanging from his lips
    bored
    Suddenly he saw a cluster of people
There! there! he shouted
    pointing for the pilot
    no longer bored
    his machine gun cocked
    and when they circled close enough
    to see the faces
    he killed! he killed!

I woke in a sweat
    (blood?)
    frightened, frightened,
    and
I wondered why he looked so much like me.

Joan, meanwhile, got herself included in a debate over
the legalization of marijuana in Mrs. Wagner's English
class, volunteering to take the affirmative side in opposition to Bruce Conway. "We talked about it," Bruce
said. "She was such a broad-minded girl, I got the feeling
we would end up more in agreement on the issue. I didn't
really know her well before that. Here she was, a cheerleader, very pretty and all, and she was talking so seriously about how so many things were wrong about society, how she couldn't understand that people could hate
each other because they were black, say, or Jewish. But
they did, you heard it enough around Blackwood. She
also thought that poverty was terrible, and that some

people didn't have enough to eat; she couldn't understand how that could be allowed. She got all worked up over it. Then she mentioned the war, but she just couldn't even get started about that. I never knew a cheerleader like her."

"Joan talked about that debate," Desi said. "She really didn't know much about it. Like she was afraid pot was a bad thing, that maybe it led to shooting heroin. I laughed. I told her it didn't any more than kissing led to pregnancy."

In his room, Craig wrestled with his gathering depression and began to fantasize with an increasing morbidity.

> The light of a street lamp shines ominously
>   through my window
> Warning me of the piercing loneliness
> I seem to be doomed with
> It stands steadfast, watching possibly waiting
> For someone to rescue it from its humility
> Perhaps someday it will
> Rescue this pitiful Christ
> from its cross
> Just as someday I will
> Be rescued from my seemingly
> Endless sorrow.

Then, on another night:

> At night I walk
> searching
> perhaps for answers
> perhaps for someone else who is searching
> The pattern of my footsteps
> may weave for me what is real
> what is important?
> The only truth I know is loneliness.

"Craig was changing," Stanley noted. "Anyone could tell he wasn't very happy about it, but who doesn't get down at times? One night, though, I went to Philly to meet my friends at a coffeehouse. I'd taken Craig there before and he liked it. But this was around one-thirty in the morning, on a weekday night, and suddenly he walked in! I really jumped, it seemed so fantastic. He said he couldn't sleep and felt down. Lonely, he said. He'd sneaked out of his house while everyone was sleeping and hopped a ride.

"We sat around rapping till real late. Craig sat there and listened; he didn't say too much. I was thinking how he'd better catch an early bus because he'd sure catch hell if he wasn't home by the time his father woke up."

It was a time when Craig and Joan apparently found themselves trapped in the ambivalence of their withdrawal, wanting it, yes, but also needing the love of others. "They seemed strange at times," said Debbie Gliick, "like they were all washed out. Once, Joan sat staring off into nowhere for the longest time and her face was so sad, I didn't know what to say. . . ."

And Craig, locked in his spiraling depression, wrote more and more to record it:

> Oh please come the day
> When I can believe
> That we must feel sorrow
> To appreciate love and beauty
> Right now, it seems not worth it
> I'm so sorry, so sorry.

Periodically, there would be attempts at rejuvenation, a little too enthusiastic, even a little desperate. There was the time, near the end of September, when Joan suggested a snipe hunt, of all things (that old American ruse), and talked it up at school for the following Saturday night. There were inevitably gullible classmates who were ready to try bagging a few snipes and the word of it spread rapidly. Curiously, what was intended to be a small party grew to mammoth proportions, several dozen cars out on Bloody Bucket Road, with any number of kids beating sticks together, burlap sacks tucked under their arms, crying out, "Here, snipe; here, snipe!" Perhaps because of its size, the group became fragmented and lost the spirit of its mutual playfulness, and what began as a party ended as a jokeless melee. It was a trival matter, a happening that didn't turn out quite right, perhaps, but it did not sit well with Craig and Joan. They wanted more unity from everyone, a greater sense of oneness and community pleasure.

"I noticed them later that night," recalled Bruce Conway. "Craig had a flat tire and we helped him change it in the dark. He wasn't sullen or anything, but he didn't smile the way he usually does, he hardly said anything."

"It was sort of dumb, I guess, and nobody cared much about the evening," Stanley said. "But Craig was upset by it. He always tried to bring people together. You just couldn't tell him that most of the kids were jerks. He just wouldn't listen to that. He really believed that people had to love each other, that there was no other workable way to live. Even on a snipe hunt."

" 'Love' was a special word to them," added Debbie. "Joan used to say that they seldom used it to each other, that they wanted to use it in the larger sense, what all people should feel for each other. It was sort of a religious thing with them."

"I asked Joan, 'How was the snipe hunt?' " Desi said. "She said she wouldn't have been surprised if someone had actually caught one of those poor little creatures. Later, she let out one of those long sighs, and then she said something about how we were a bunch of snipe hunters in Vietnam, thrashing through the jungle killing and burning out those people. You could see the wheels turning around in her head, and then she looked at me with such sadness. 'What are we going to do?' she said."

8

October 1969. Fifty million American boys and girls had returned to school, but halfway around the world, a cruel, uninspiring war hung endlessly over their lives. If the educational process was designed to gratify society's need to control adolescents, for the first time there was an overriding fear that students, when massed together, were potentially less controllable than when on the loose. War was always the special horror of the young, perhaps more so in America—where only the young did the dying, while adults espouse patriotism and prosper in the process—the only leading country in the Western world that had not suffered a modern invasion or bombing attack. However, to the children who have grown up in an age of nuclear bombs and ballistic missiles, America's historical invulnerability had no meaning whatsoever.

It wasn't only the children—there were millions of adults who had come to the same conclusion—but it was essentially the demands of youth that powered the dramatic drive to Moratorium Day, October 15.

It had begun in April, in Boston, an idea in the mind of a wealthy, middle-aged envelope manufacturer named Jerome Grossman. His concept was a one-day nationwide strike for peace, to stop the entire economy of America in a giant protest against the Vietnam war. His colleague was Sam Brown, aged twenty-six, a student leader half his age. ("The student leaders of today will be the student leaders of tomorrow" went the popular adage.) Brown objected to the notion of, and the word, "strike" and offered the idea of a moratorium instead. Moratorium, according to one dictionary definition: "A temporary cessation of activity, especially of an activity considered hostile or dangerous." The date first set for mid-

September was later delayed for a month to give students more time to organize.

The responses were, at first, cautious and unencouraging. It wasn't until well into September that the organizing drive began in earnest. As it turned out, the period was a fertile one, far more so than any of them dared to predict. The country that had supported President Nixon's Vietnam policies in June was overwhelmingly opposing them in September. Support for the demonstrations came from a wide variety of sources. As *Time* magazine described it: "Small-town housewives and Wall Street lawyers, college presidents and politicians, veteran demonstrators and people who had never made the V sign of the peace movement planned to turn out on 'M Day' to register their dismay and frustration over Vietnam."

On September 26, the President himself gave the movement a new thrust with a statement he would later regret: ". . . under no circumstances will I be affected whatever by the antiwar protests." And a few days later, he added that Americans did not "buckle and run away, but stood fast, so that the enemy knew it had no choice but to negotiate." At the same time he precluded the possibility of any real negotiation by saying he would not be the first President to preside over a United States military defeat—negotiated or otherwise.

For weeks, the action around the peace movement would dominate the news leading up to the Moratorium, and everything written seemed to aggrandize it. It was no trumped-up happening, but right in the viscera of America's anguish, and no community in the mainstream could be totally free of its impact.

Even Blackwood, New Jersey, was touched, for all its efforts to the contrary. There were no radical groups in the area, no chapters of any peace organizations, no organized student groups of protest, no known militants among its few blacks. The local newspaper reflected the mores and values of the silent majority of its contented citizens, its representative in Congress (John Hunt, First District) was truly representative, and the ministers of its many and varied churches conducted themselves accordingly.

At Highland High, the coming of the Moratorium created barely a ripple. There were a few, like Desi Worland, who picked up a batch of antiwar literature from her friends in Philadelphia and attempted to distribute leaflets in and around school. "I was stopped several times. They told me it was not allowed on school grounds. It was truly incredible, how ignorant everyone was. We were just a few miles outside of Philly, and nobody had the slightest idea what was going on in the country. There was hardly a student who had even heard of SDS, for instance. You mention the Weathermen, and they think it's the guys they see on the TV news, forecasting the weather."

"Silence," said Stanley. "The teachers were nice, some were very nice; they'd let you talk about things sometimes, but what they really preferred was silence."

"They'd conduct a discussion about the war," added Desi, "but they couldn't get past a certain point they'd read in a textbook or *Life* magazine, maybe. It had to be safe, everything according to the rules. Every idea had to come out of some book endorsed by the system. It was a joke. Like in our social studies class, Mr. Towers was saying how great the American penal system was, and I jumped all over him. 'Wait a minute!' I cried out. I knew better, firsthand, and when I started telling them what it was really like, everyone ran scared. It isn't what they're supposed to think, and when someone says it isn't true, they feel threatened. The government says the war is necessary, so they go along with it. You don't lose your job agreeing with the government. They just don't know any better."

"I really couldn't understand how so many students supported the war, or just didn't care," said Liz Quemore. "They took a poll and barely twenty per cent opposed it! And the teachers, they were the same as the students. I *never* heard a teacher speak out against the war. Some actively spoke in favor of it, opposing the Moratorium for example. They called it unpatriotic, and they made it terribly clear in class that last week. . . ."

Craig had reacted to the first reports of the coming big day in a very positive way. He had never been politically oriented, but this, at last, had sparked him. The idea of a nationwide demonstration to concretize a protest against killing was a beautiful expression of humanity. "He would read everything he could find about it," Bernie said. "We would talk about it, frequently even in the presence of Mom and Dad. Craig wanted them to know how he felt, hoping he could get Dad to understand. He wanted their support, and he was willing to risk an argument to make his point. He was tired of suppressing his thoughts at home; he didn't want to do that any more."

Bernie's wife said: "Craig was becoming much more political at home. The Vietnam war had made him more aware. We discussed it in the larger sense, how it had become part of American life, not just an involvement sixteen thousand miles away, how it touched everyone's values. He was appalled at certain incidents, the napalming, the bombing of civilians, the destruction of villages. He would ask: 'What for? Why are we doing this?' Sure, he knew the official answers, but he just couldn't accept any political interpretations that justified this sort of murder."

At school, he became annoyed at the insensitiveness of his teachers and fellow students, for it was with them that he faced the test of his expanding opinions. His battleground was at Highland Regional High School, not the Mekong Delta, and he waged a persistent and dedicated assault on their indifference. As noted by his friend Stanley, "He kept saying we had to do something to help them," referring to his peers. One day, in history class, there was a discussion about the treatment of Viet Cong prisoners, and reference was made to an American Marine technique of questioning suspects by suspending them by the heels from flying helicopters: if they refused to talk, they were dropped. Said teacher David Towers: "The mention of this attracted a certain amount of laughter in class, mostly, I suppose, out of embarrassment. But Craig was immediately upset. He cried out for them to stop, that it was a terrible thing for them to laugh at. 'That's the trouble,' he said. 'We can't take it seriously enough to really understand.' Everyone became silent at once; it was a very moving moment."

Craig was relentless and forceful, but always considerate and never provocative. When he heard a boy boasting about how he had met a soldier back from Vietnam who had been decorated for having killed twelve "gooks," Craig asked him to consider who he thought was really better off for it. "The guy looked at Craig," Stanley recalled, "and he couldn't figure out if Craig was crazy or what. Craig wouldn't let him go. He said: 'Think about it; what good did it do? Are we going to have to kill them all? And what, specifically, is a "gook?"' The way he said it, it cut right through you, like suddenly you really had to stop and figure it out. The guy was embarrassed, all right. He just couldn't answer. . . ." Then Stanley added: "One thing about Craig, he had guts. He was no coward when it came to speaking his mind."

"It was the kind of courage that brought others to think he was weird," said Charlie Kean. "You know, like the only guts that counted with them was to fight with your fists, and Craig would never do that. He thought that was barbaric."

New York Times
OCTOBER 10
The National Council of Churches, through its religious leaders, officially endorsed the Moratorium. "Never before has there been an observance in which the religious forces of the United States have been in greater accord."

During the week leading up to the Moratorium, Craig became increasingly involved in its prospects. "The whole idea of it fascinated him," Bernie said. "He began to sense the tremendous power that millions of people could generate, all over the country, people taking off from work and pouring into the streets of big cities, rallying to say, 'Stop the war!' He could feel close to people doing that, he said. He thought he would even go to Washington where it had to be even more significant. He really hoped it was going to be a big thing, an important thing."

New York Times
OCTOBER 11
Seventy-nine college heads, representing leading Amer-

ican seats of learning, signed a statement bidding
President Nixon to step up the Vietnam withdrawal
in the belief that the war was harmful to American
society.

"We talked about the Moratorium on Saturday night,"
Stanley noted. "Craig drove a gang of us over to the
Camden County Community College for a forum on
theater. On the way back, he brought it up, only it was
hard to talk in that car. He had a broken muffler or
something like that and there were gas fumes coming in
and we had to open the windows. Everyone started talking about that instead, and he said, okay, okay, he was
going to fix it the next day."

New York Times
OCTOBER 12
Four thousand demonstrators, marching eight abreast
in a cordon that stretched for over a quarter-mile,
closed in on a thousand MP's at Fort Dix, N.J., in a
protest against treatment of prisoners there. They
were dispersed by tear gas.
Meanwhile, in Washington, D.C., Secretary of State
William P. Rogers said that the rising criticism of
President Nixon's Vietnam policy had "eliminated any
possibility of a negotiated settlement to the war in
the next few months."

"He fixed the tail pipe on Sunday afternoon," Bernie
said. "He had gotten hold of a new pipe and connected
it to the muffler. I knew he had done it well because I
drove his car on that afternoon. Mine was blocked in the
driveway, and rather than go through the chore of moving the cars, I took his. I was surprised about what
happened because when I got back home, he was angry
with me. He never got angry about that sort of thing. I
was gone only a few minutes. . . ."

New York Times
OCTOBER 13
The President vowed again not to be swayed by
war protests, asserting there was ". . . nothing new

we can learn from demonstrations" in an interchange of letters with a student at Georgetown University named Randy Dicks who had written to protest Nixon's apparent indifference. Nixon replied: ". . . Others can say of Vietnam, 'get out now'; when asked how, they can give the simple flip answer: 'By sea.' But as I consider these consequences in both human and international terms, I can only conclude that history would rightly condemn a President who took such a course. . . ."

On Monday, the Highland Regional High School administration officially announced that it did not look with favor on any absences from classes because of the Peace Moratorium, even with permission from parents. Students skipping classes would have to suffer the consequences, and those missing tests would suffer a double penalty.

"You could feel how some of the teachers thought that was just great," Desi said. "They hated the Moratorium, and now they could make trouble for anybody who wanted to go."

"Our English teacher, Mrs. Richards, said she was going to give us a test on Wednesday," Debbie Gliick noted. "She said it would count double against us if we missed it, really punishing anyone for going to the Moratorium. I was horrified. I spoke up and I don't usually do that. I said to the teacher: 'You're being very closed-minded!' I was really very upset, but Craig, he didn't approve of what I did. He told me: 'You're only stirring up more controversy. Are we going to have to fight over how to be peaceful?' He wanted everyone to go to the Moratorium but he just didn't want anyone to argue about it."

"They made a concession to us if we came to school," said Stanley. "They would allow those of us who believed in the Moratorium to take off one period at the end of the day to have our own ceremony. They even allowed us twenty-four hours to organize it."

"I don't think anyone had the slightest idea how many children would absent themselves," Mrs. Betty Quemore commented, "except that the atmosphere in town was clearly opposed to it. You heard more talk about people

flying flags or driving cars with the headlights on than
sharing rides to Glassboro [the site of the nearest rally]
or Philly. You could guess that most of the kids would
go to school as usual, but the school people were worried. All of my kids came home with reports of how
teachers were putting the pressure on."

On Monday night, Craig and Joan visited Mark Bunzell. If either was depressed, it was not evident. "They
just dropped in, nothing unusual about it," Mark said.
"They talked about the Moratorium and I asked if I
could go with them, but they said they'd planned to go
alone. It didn't seem strange and I didn't question it.
Craig and I watched TV. 'Laugh-In.' Joan was helping
my kid sister with her homework. She really liked Joan,
like she would go to the football games just to cheer
Joan. We used to kid her about that—cheering for the
cheerleader and not the team. It was a routine pleasant
visit, really." And Mark would have to wonder: "I just
don't see how, two nights later, they could have gotten
to that point. . . ."

Craig wrote:

> And so it goes these days and nights
> that lead me to my constant sorrow
> Where I'll just drift and quiet pass
> And wish and hope for love tomorrow.

Still, he had Joan. She loved him and she was always
there for him. He felt her love and knew how vital it
was, how much of her was devoted to him. If this, as it
turned out, actually bothered him, for he did not share
her all-encompassing emotion, nonetheless he loved her
in return. "I love her, yes," he had told Desi. "I know I
will always love her. It's such a fantastic thing to think
about." To Joan, however, her involvement with Craig
was so complete it made less of everything else. As Gail
Hillias had put it: "Joan was very nearly obsessed by
him." Craig, however, wanted to be a man in the entire
world around him, to find a way to live with others that
could gratify his infinite need for brotherhood.

If I could feel the love of others

I would not grieve so much
I reach out for them
   in a way they do not understand.
I need them because they are my brothers
   but they do not seem to need anyone.
And that is the loneliest thing of all.

New York Times
OCTOBER 14
In Washington, over twenty Congressmen planned
an all-night vigil in the halls of Congress, an open
debate on the issues of the war.

"We were walking out to the parking lot after school
on Tuesday," Stanley recalled. "Craig wanted to know
who was going to do what on Moratorium Day. Some
creep said how it was all a lot of nonsense begun by a
bunch of long-haired freaks in New York City who go
around waving the Viet Cong flag. Craig tried to reason
with him, telling him that a lot of people wanted the war
to end and this would be a good way to show it. Then
someone else said it wouldn't show anything much, just
a bunch of kids using it as an excuse to cut school—
like they wanted to watch the World Series on TV.
Then a girl put in that her brother was going to be
drafted next month and she didn't see how it was anything but unpatriotic to demonstrate against the government. There were like fifteen or twenty kids standing
around us and it seemed like all of them were telling
Craig how they were opposed to the Moratorium or
couldn't have cared less. But he stood there battling it
out. In the end, all he could ask was, didn't they think
the war was a terrible thing. The horror of it was, they
said no, not really, and one of them gave the brilliant
answer that it was a necessary part of history, he
even quoted Clausewitz, and that if it weren't, how come
we keep on having them!"

New York Times
OCTOBER 14
In London, fifty MP's introduced a motion in the

House of Commons expressing full support for American war protesters.

In New York, Mayor John V. Lindsay planned to deck City Hall in mourning and lower all flags to half-mast.

In Hanoi, *Nhan Dan,* official North Vietnam newspaper, published a letter from Premier Phan Van Dong in which he stated his enthusiastic approval of the Moratorium, calling the American demonstrators "our heroic comrades-in-arms."

In Washington, the Nixon Administration used this letter in hopes of embarrassing those Congressmen sympathetic to the coming day. As Vice President Spiro T. Agnew suggested: Did not this letter from Hanoi make the whole Moratorium suspect?

"I spoke to Craig that afternoon," Desi noted. "He was feeling down. There were all these straight friends of his who meant so much to him and they didn't understand what he was going through . . . the typical Blackwood kids. They wouldn't do anything that might make waves."

He drove off with Joan that Tuesday afternoon, and no one knew where they went or what they did. They were alone together, that was normal for them. What they decided to do, finally, was anything but.

Late in the afternoon, he brought Joan to her home in time for dinner, and returned home himself. "It was early that evening," Bernie recalled, "I walked by Craig's room and saw him writing letters. There was a batch of airmail envelopes scattered across his desk. I stood there, a few feet away, and asked him if he wanted to go out with Margie and me, we were going to visit my aunt's. He thought about it for a minute or two, and then said no, he had some things to do.

"Thinking back, I don't know how he could have been so cool. Even his voice. It was cheerful. He didn't have the slightest tremor in his voice. He was sitting there writing those suicide notes and there was absolutely nothing about him that suggested it."

When he finished, he cleared out his desk. Notes, stories, letters, poems. He rummaged through his closet for the bound notebooks of his writings that dated back for years. He gathered them all together, took them outside to the incinerator in the back yard, and burned them.

Joan, meanwhile, was writing letters of her own.

9

Glassboro is a small town barely fifteen minutes south of Blackwood, the seat of a Jersey State College that dominates the life of the community. It was not without historical significance that a Moratorium rally was held here. In June 1967, it was the site of a world-famous meeting between President Lyndon Johnson and Soviet Premier Aleksei Kosygin, ostensibly to discuss those pressure points that separated the two leading world powers and effect a rapprochement that would cement the peace. It was the first such meeting between the two, and the entire world sensed that history was hanging in the balance. Glassboro itself was overwhelmed by the significance of it, though it was chosen by geographical accident, being midway between New York and Washington. Not only students gathered on that notable afternoon, but residents too, lingering on a grassy hilltop outside the ivied buildings, first in the broiling sun and then through a torrential downpour, waiting for a glimpse of the two that they might somehow give vent to what was in their hearts. And when the two emerged from their meeting, there suddenly erupted a stirring cry that reverberated off the buildings with an astounding impact. "We want peace, we want peace . . ." Over and over they chanted, several thousand voices, and the two most powerful men in the world waved and smiled and nodded, and some said there were tears in Mr. Johnson's eyes.

On Wednesday, October 15, 1969, almost two and a half years later, over four thousand assembled again. A larger crowd this time—indeed, the largest crowd that Glassboro had ever seen. It was a young crowd, mainly students, many from nearby towns. They were mostly a neat, middle-class crowd, though others were long-haired, bearded, blue-jeaned kids. They were an amiable, unsophisticated group, most of whom had never been to such a demonstration before and did not know how to act or what to expect. It was not like the typical patriotic rallies they had known on a Fourth of July, no brass bands and military parades or floats with official pomp. They were gathered in the autumn sunshine and they stood around waiting to be told what to do and where to go. In time there was a march to the site of the ceremonies where speeches were made and songs were sung.

Craig and Joan had arrived early and found themselves wandering aimlessly, more as spectators than participants, as they waited for the program to begin. The lack of organization distressed them. They had come for inspiration and they saw only chaos.

"I could see how they might feel dispirited," said Liz Quemore. "There were small groups of kids scattered around doing their thing, a couple here and there making out under a tree, others playing guitar and singing, and there were some with transistors listening to the World Series and every once in a while you'd hear someone holler out the score and cheer for the Mets. The problem was, the program itself was not well organized. It was the old business about getting a permit to march on Main Street, that sort of mess. Town officials always seem to make it difficult, if not impossible, to set it up properly. They keep everything up in the air until the last minute. Then they say, contemptuously, that peace groups are so disorganized."

Whatever Craig and Joan might have been looking for, they did not find it at Glassboro. Although they had made their suicide pact, they had left the door open, hoping to find a new level of experience on this day that might dissuade them from their commitment.

"After the march, we saw them sitting a few yards in front of us," Liz said. "Craig turned and happened to look back and our eyes met. I thought maybe I ought to ask them to join us, but since he was with Joan, I thought better of it. Then he turned away and it struck me how miserable he seemed. I mean, like he was suffering terribly. It hit me so, I couldn't help thinking how much I still liked him."

They left early and returned to Blackwood, stopping at school around three-fifteen to pick up some things from their lockers. "I ran into Craig in the hall," Mark Bunzell said. "I asked him how the Moratorium went. He wasn't too happy about it; too many kids were there just to have a good time, he said. There wasn't enough 'true feeling.' He wanted to talk, I could tell. He sort of leaned against a locker to get comfortable, but I had a band rehearsal and I didn't want to be late. He looked at me so strangely, I didn't know what to do. It was a kind of special 'I'm sorry' look, like he was apologizing, maybe. I suspected something was wrong, but I really had to go. I remember walking away from him, not liking it at all. . . ."

Gail Hillias saw Joan in school and heard much the same story. "It had not been an inspiring day for them. Joan said something about how a lot of the kids there seemed more interested in how the Mets were doing than what the speakers were trying to say."

At around three-thirty, they went up to Mrs. Wagner's home room, but did not find her there. They waited for a while, then finally scrawled a note on the blackboard. Mrs. Wagner, tied up in a meeting, did not get back to her room until some time later, and barely took heed of the message. "We waited for you. Craig and Joan." It was only the next day that she would grieve over it, wondering what, actually, they had come to say to her, and by how many minutes she had missed them.

Craig dropped off Joan, arranging to pick her up at seven that evening, then returned home. Both had a number of things to do, last letters to write. However, there would be no farewells, no dramatics, no anxious moment in front of others.

"It was too bad they left Glassboro so early," Liz commented. "The finale was around five. Thousands of us, all together finally, singing, 'All we are saying is give peace a chance.' It was really very moving."

"I had a job at RCA in Haddonfield at the time," Bernie said. "I'd arranged to pick up a remnant there; I needed a carpet for my apartment upstairs. I saw Craig about five, or five-thirty, and we discussed the Glassboro scene for a minute or two. He shrugged it off

as nothing special. He was sitting with his back to me,
shining his shoes, and one of the very few times I ever
did this—and I don't really know why—I laid a hand on
his shoulder, a loving kind of thing to do. I said I wondered if he would help me unload the carpet, help me
lay it upstairs because it would probably be too heavy
for me. He replied that he wouldn't be here. He was
going to pick up Joan and go back to Glassboro for
the candlelight march, that everyone was saying how
that would be the best part of the day.

"But there *was* a hesitancy in his voice. In retrospect,
I think he wanted to tell me, I really think he did. It was
such a normal scene, though. We were always shining our
shoes, the same sort of plain brown shells we always
wore, never out of style. I just didn't react.

"It was the last time I ever spoke with him."

Shortly after Bernie left for the carpet, their mother
received a phone call from her father, Jesse Ivins, reporting that his wife was not feeling well. As a result,
Dolly Badiali decided that she would skip her regular
Wednesday night Weight Watchers meeting. Craig, hearing the end of this communication, was immediately
concerned. Was Grandma all right? His mother assured
him that it wasn't anything serious, but he didn't believe
her . . . if everything was all right, then why wasn't she
going to the Weight Watchers?

As Bernie had said, it was a normal scene.

It was their last confrontation with him, this touching
display of selflessness. He was about to kill himself, but
news that his aging grandmother might not be feeling
well could pull him up short.

He sat at his desk and finished writing the twelve letters, several to his immediate family—at that moment
sitting in rooms a few yards away. It was after six-thirty
when he began a final note to his closest friend, Frank
DiGenova up at RPI in Troy, New York.

 . . . I waited until last to write you.

      My life is complete except all my brothers are
in trouble—war, poverty, hunger, hostility.

My purpose is to make them understand all this trouble.

Maybe this will start a chain reaction of awakening, love, communication.

I've been so down, so goddam down, I can't get up. Not even pot helps.

Read my poetry and make people understand how I feel. Make them tell each other how beautiful they are.

Take my life into yours.

If I sound strange, it's because I am insane with sorrow and distress.

Please make them see!

Love and peace, Craig.

He sealed the last envelope and wrote "Frank DiGenova" on its face. Sometime around seven, he left his room for the last time. For the most part, he had cleared it out the day before. He had long since emptied a large glass water-cooler jar of the pennies he had been saving for pocket money, and brought it to Margie, a gift for Matthew. His walls, formerly covered with posters, signs, pop art, and all the usual teen-age decorations, were bare; he had stripped and burned these with his papers the day before. Only one item remained—a sign: "DON'T GO AWAY MAD—JUST GO AWAY."

He climbed the short stairwell to the kitchen and saw his father at the table, the only one left at home, leafing through the evening newspaper over a cup of coffee. Craig lingered for a moment to say good night, nervously fingering the strings of his guitar. Bernard reached into his pocket to withdraw an unsolicited five dollars—"for gas," he said—then said he hoped the evening would go well, and that he should be home before midnight.

Craig nodded his thanks and left.

Joan spent a lot of time in the early evening on the phone with Desi, waiting for Craig. "She was depressed about everything, especially after the Moratorium. I tried to cheer her up, telling her it was all part of the peace movement, all kinds of people, and that it does help, even though they might have acted silly. I told her how great it was in Philly, how thousands of people jammed into the Square, kids and housewives and businessmen, how Philly had never been as crowded with as many people together in a ceremony like that. She said she had to hang up because Craig was coming and she wasn't quite ready, that they were going to Glassboro again for the candlelight march. I tried to tell her that everything would come out all right, it really would, because people wanted peace. She said, 'Well, maybe so, if I live that long. . . .'"

They didn't drive to Glassboro, but directly to Chew's Landing and the dirt road along the Big Timber Creek called Bee's Lane. It was dark and isolated, a road seldom used, especially at night. Indeed, it was known to hardly any of the kids. Craig parked his car under a cluster of buttonwood trees and removed the vacuum cleaner hose from the trunk. He attached it to the new tail pipe he had inserted on Sunday, then ran it up through a hole under the floor matting in the back seat. Later, Thomas Daley, the coroner, would say that he had drilled that hole, but it had not been necessary: his 1962 Falcon had been built with two large metal plugs, easily removable for drainage in the event of flooding. He had done this as part of his repair work on Sunday. (It is also likely that he first discovered those plugs at that time, relieving him of any need to drill. Curiously, a few days before, he had asked Mrs. Wagner, of all people, if she had a drill that he might borrow. The question struck her as odd and she referred him to the school shop. She did not recall asking what he wanted it for. "It was one of those strange questions a boy will ask sometimes: 'You wouldn't happen to have a drill, now, would you?'—that sort of thing. I didn't think about it until after I'd read the coroner's report. . . .")

The two guitars remained on the floor in the rear, the twenty-four letters in a pile on the dashboard. Craig removed the faded army jacket he was wearing in the evening chill and laid it on the back seat. Then they rolled up the windows as tightly as possible, and in time, he turned on the ignition.

In a very few minutes, the oxygen in the car was poisoned by the thrust of carbon monoxide, thick with black soot from the filthy engine. Within a very few minutes, Craig slumped against the window, his head pressing against the glass, and Joan fell lifeless against his shoulder.

10

The earliest recorded occupancy of the South Jersey area derives from the *Leni-lenapes,* "The Original People," as their Indian name translates, a remarkable tribe with an intriguing history. Beginning around 800 B.C., it is recorded that the Lenapes began a gargantuan migration that took them across Asia, the Bering Strait, then south and east across Canada and the United States, until, in 1396, their King Wolemenap (translation: Hollow Man) brought them to a wilderness of gently rolling pine-covered slopes and open fields that led from a beautiful river (the Delaware) to the Atlantic shore.

They were splendid men, strong in physique, broad-shouldered, slim-waisted, dark-eyed, pure white of teeth, wearing coarse black hair of which only a single tuft remained on top (to accommodate an enemy's scalping blade?). Their occupancy of the territory brought them joy and abundance. Deer and rabbit were plentiful as were fish and Crustaceans. They learned to grow vegetables, corn, beans, sweet potatoes, to supplement the wild berries, nuts, and fruits that surrounded them. They made weapons of stone, utensils of copper, pottery of clay. They created paints and dyes, and fashioned clothing of skins in an artful style. They built canoes by felling trees, hollowing them by gouging and burning, then covering them with protective bark.

When the Dutch found them in the early seventeenth century, there were approximately eight thousand Lenapes, friendly and hospitable, sharing food and land with the white man, absorbing much of the white man's culture that inevitably included whisky and smallpox—the two principal factors in their eventual decimation. The British continued the process, and by the time of the American

Revolutionary War, there were very few left, having been pushed westward by the expanding needs of the colonists, first into Pennsylvania and Ohio where they were Christianized and, on occasion, massacred. Those surviving continued trekking westward and settled as far away as Oklahoma.

According to Stewart English, an aging Blackwoodian with a passion for local history, the early Lenapes would come south from Trenton to summer at the shore near what was to become Atlantic City, leaving their old and sick with local tribes; as a result, many were buried in the Blackwood area. Contemporaries of Craig Badiali, who grew up in the area along Big Timber Creek and the vast farm lands that surrounded it, used to find arrowheads in their wanderings. There were others, more recently even, who have watched the bulldozers clearing the foliage for new housing developments, and found arrowheads churned up by the giant blades.

The history of the area now known as Gloucester Township dates back to 1699, when a man named Richard Chew sailed from England and eventually brought his small, sturdy craft up the Delaware River to the north branch of the Big Timber Creek. It is said that Mrs. Chew had him put ashore at that point, enchanted by the sight of a vast number of goldfinch. More probably, it was the excellent harbor that attracted the captain, who purchased over six hundred acres and began the village of Chew's Landing. At the time, the creek was a broad, deep channel capable of floating ocean-going craft, and the landing became the site of considerable shipbuilding and harbor activities.

The village prospered from the beginning, largely because of the John Blackwood farm, just a few miles away. This was, on record, the oldest settlement in the Township of Gloucester and was appropriately named Blackwood in 1740. The original road between Chew's Landing and Blackwood was the Old Black Horse Pike, and after a number of resurfacing jobs over the centuries, it still exists. It was used then by John Blackwood to bring produce to Chew's Landing for shipment to Philadelphia.

In 1789, while colonial troops were en route to Trenton,

George Washington himself came to Chew's Landing. It is said that he and a number of his men found lodging at the Chew's Landing Tavern, a well-kept inn owned and operated by Aaron Chew. After a night of excessive drinking, however, the men were apparently unfit for duty and General Washington was properly miffed. He sought out Captain Chew, asking why he had permitted such conduct in his establishment. Though Chew was unable to reply, one of his townspeople spoke in his defense:

"The Captain could not help the conduct of your men, General; but perhaps if we had a church of God here, deeds like this could be properly forgiven," whereupon Washington was solicited for a contribution to the building of the first Saint John's Episcopal Church. The official records list his contribution at fifteen shillings.

Both the tavern and the adjacent church flourished, especially the former, which became famous for fine food, excellent ale, and warm hospitality, while the church was the center of Sunday activities and all the social action of the community not special to the tavern. It was a time when the people worshiped with a great zeal, for they believed it was the providence of the Lord that made a man or a community prosperous. The small stone structure came to be revered by its congregants, who were proud of its hand-fashioned pine pews and the large brass cross heading the altar, which was always polished to a magnificent high shine.

A fine fishing and swimming area was located barely a quarter mile away at the northern tip of the Big Timber Creek, and in the warm Jersey summers, it was the center of daytime recreation. It came to be called The Buttonball, named after the buttonwood trees that lined its shores. Mothers would bring small children to be bathed in its clear water. Barely five miles upstream, Walt Whitman, a native of Camden, was a frequent visitor to pack his arthritic limbs in the mud of these same therapeutic waters, the exact spot of his choosing now marked as a shrine.

Today, the Big Timber Creek has become so polluted, the kids say "you can walk across it." There are no fish in the historic creek, and no boats cruise along its shallow waterway. Indeed, it is no longer a landing but a decaying memory of rotting logs overhanging a small polluted stream. There are those still alive who remember its better days, like Craig Badiali's grandfather, Jesse Ivins, himself a craftsman who worked on ships. "It all began to crumble around here after World War II, and nobody seemed to care. They were building these new developments all along the Timber Creek and moving the earth this way and that, and pouring Lord knows what junk into those waters. It got so it seemed to shrivel up right before your eyes. And now you could hardly move a two-man canoe down to the Landing. . . ."

And the old Chew's Tavern, now called the Chew's Landing Hotel Tavern, is a dilapidated building of sadly weathered clapboard and decaying drainage pipes; inside a visitor is greeted by the pungent smell of yesterday's beer and bathroom deodorants and the neon signs over the long wooden bar. The Tavern has known over thirty owners since Aaron Chew, during which time the disintegrating process has been relentless. It is said that during its turbulent history, the hotel would play host to the South Jersey Mafiosi in Prohibition days. There are also reports that it was the scene of more than one explosive gangster shoot-out.

There are still eighteenth-century relics gathering dust on the inner walls, but no one pays attention to them. If it was, indeed, a place where George Washington had slept, the current site of such an historic occasion is hardly worthy of it, though they call the inner tavern the Washington Room—a collection of small tables on a soiled floor where a weekend dance band collects local revelers. "The Hotel," reads its most recent biography, "has always moved with the trend of the times. The first television set ever seen in Chew's Landing was seen at the Hotel."

Up until World War II, the geographical entity that included Blackwood, Chew's Landing, and a dozen other unclassified communities was quiet, sparsely settled, maintaining its tradition of agriculture. The ethnic stock remained primarily British and Dutch with roots many generations deep. Their religious affiliations were exclusively Protestant; there were no Catholic churches or Jewish temples. Nor were there more than a handful of blacks, who had settled a few miles away, relatively isolated in a community known as Erial. There were no wealthy people in the area; indeed, in all its history, rich people went elsewhere, settling in nearby enclaves such as Haddonfield, Collingswood, and most recently, Cherry Hill. Yet there was a pleasant old simplicity about Blackwood and its environs. Old houses, well preserved, on farmlike acreage. The Badialis and the Ivinses lived that way. Sprawling farms, undulating across broad open plains, surrounded them. There was little traffic in the shopping areas, and living was uncomplicated by the pressures of excessive ambition and the obvious inequities of vast class differences. The community ethic was in the best American tradition: hard work, thrift, honesty, devotion to God. As late as 1950, there were scarcely more than six thousand people in the area and very little industry. Ten years later, the population had almost doubled, but was easily absorbed, with no interruption in the mode of living. However, the handwriting of change was on the wall and old natives began to brace themselves for what appeared to be the inevitable. Nearby Philadelphia was bursting at the seams, rendering a pleasant family existence impossible. To the white workingman who found himself suddenly affluent in the postwar years, there was no achievement greater than ownership of a home of his own in the suburbs, especially in the face of increasingly troublesome confrontations with dissident urban blacks. Then in the 1960s, thousands of blue collar workers, mostly Italian and Irish, fled the city and came to such communities as Blackwood where new and inexpensive homes were waiting for them on pleasantly curving tree-lined streets. The population of the newly activated political entity known as Gloucester Township multiplied rapidly until at the 1970 census, it was close to twenty-five thousand—well over half of whom had arrived within the previous five years.

Almost overnight, everything underwent an extraordinary change. Huge new building developments like Timberline (five hundred homes), Glen Oaks (eight hundred homes), Somerdale, new apartment complexes, and dozens of smaller tracts. The neighborhood grocery was replaced by huge chain supermarkets like A&P, 7-11, Acme, and a dozen franchise hamburger stands like MacDonald's, Burger Chef, and White Tower dominated the Black Horse Pike. There was a minor influx of industry: Foremost Milk opened up a dairy plant; Hyde Plastics and Sun Temp Heating Corporation built large factories just off the Thruway that penetrated Blackwood.

The main artery through the entire township is the Black Horse Pike, named after its historic forebear, running south from the outskirts of Camden into Washington Township. Its approach to Blackwood from Camden runs through such postal areas as Bellmawr, Glendora, Runnemede, Blenheim, Hilltop, several miles of gas stations and used-car lots, car-wash and hamburger stands. The principal eatery is a large diner, though a few neighboring taverns serve pizza and several Italian specialties. The two or three blocks that constitute the core of Blackwood support a more tightly enclosed shopping district of established shops: a drug store, bank, tailor shop, hobby shop, florist shop (owned by a descendant of the Chew family), movie theater, and liquor store, all surrounding a single traffic light at the juncture of Church Street and the Pike that marks the center of town.

Along the narrow streets that seem hidden from the Pike, there are quiet residential areas, old homes built a few yards from the road, as was the custom in the days before automobiles. Fine old maples and oaks tower over them, supplying shade and beauty to many streets. A few blocks west of the Pike, Church Street crosses a railroad track, the remains of the old single track, the "Peanut Line," as it was called, once carrying commuters from nearby Grenloch into Camden some fifteen miles north, and thence into Philadelphia across the Delaware River. Behind this defunct line, the old Blackwood Lake lies dormant and unused, another relic of the tranquil times before population and pollution desecrated the simple pleasures of the community. This body of water, like the Big Timber Creek that runs into Chew's Landing, is also looked upon contemptuously by residents, many of whom were present when one could swim in it.

In an area of such rapid expansion, there is neither homogeneity nor local pride. Nor are there concerted attempts to instill any by the local city fathers. It has become a polyglot community of different ethnic groups from varying religious persuasions, and for the most part, they have settled into their own enclaves ostensibly to live and let live, as peacefully as possible. The truth is, they have succeeded in effecting this as a proper *modus vivendi*, and there has been a very minimum of friction—and just as little commingling and friendly communication. Only the kids are in contact with each other in the schools, but even there the progress of their friendships—especially in the younger, preadolescent years—seems to vary directly with the distance between their homes. As for the blacks, almost all of whom live in Erial, their exclusion from the mainstream of local social life is all but complete—again, even in the schools, despite all the politeness that many whites are able to maintain. The unwritten though not unspoken rule is one of segregation, and there is peace among the races largely because blacks are so few in number. Typically, several black families have managed to penetrate the new ornate development at Glen Oaks; they are four out of eight hundred. This is perhaps the only area generating a pride of community—and that, for primarily snobbish reasons.

Through it all, however, there is a remarkable continuity of the old law-abiding traditions that have prevailed through the turbulence of the postwar years. There is almost no crime in Blackwood to properly occupy its twenty-two-man police force. Young people cannot remember the case of any local homicide, nor even a crime of passion. There are no problems of stolen cars or breaking and entering, or, for that matter, any of the criminality one is apt to find in the more affluent suburbs contiguous to New York City. Bernie Badiali recalls how, when he was a teen-ager, he engaged in a mischievous plan with some friends to make winter use of an idle summer house of unknown ownership. "It was just for an adventure, you might say; we never took or messed up anything." But when it was discovered, the police descended upon the Badiali household as though a hardened criminal were in their midst. Even today, residents of Blackwood seldom lock their doors except when they leave town for a few days, nor do they take keys from their cars when they park in the neighborhood.

The normally present problems of juvenile delinquency are almost nonexistent. A juvenile board meets every week to help those troubled youths who might be brought before them. There are very few. Members of the clergy will pridefully account for this phenomenon by referring to the continued strength of the family unit that has been maintained here while in other, more urban communities, it has failed.

At the same time, there is no community youth activity outside the church and the home, though there is a considerable demand for it. Teen-agers legitimately complain that there are too few places for them to gather, and certainly none that are specifically designed for them. A youth association was established in 1968 under the aegis of sympathetic adults like Mrs. Betty Quemore, hoping to establish a local coffeehouse where kids might congregate for music and talk. It was eventually stopped by town fathers who found that certain local ordinances allegedly rendered such a place illegal. Actually, the idea of a teen-age hangout was far too threatening for many of them. And "coffeehouse," apparently, had conspiratorial implications built into its very name.

Blackwood has, essentially, a church-going population, closely identified with old-fashioned Fundamentalist religiosity. There are over a dozen churches, most of them well attended on Sunday as well as for numerous midweek social functions. Their impact is a stabilizing force for the maintenance of the status quo in all aspects of community life.

Most of the men now residing in the area are tradesmen and small-businessmen associated with firms and construction jobs in Philadelphia, less than twenty minutes away, yet they do not use Philadelphia for cultural purposes. It could be said that, apart from work, the principal bond to the city is that of professional sports: the Phillies, Eagles, Warriors, the big three in

baseball, football, and basketball, though most of their
viewing is via television. Blackwoodians avoid the city,
seeing it as a menace, a symbol of crime and filth and
racial chaos.

Outside the home, the principal social action takes
place in an assortment of local taverns where, at spots
like the old Chew's Landing Hotel Tavern, there is live
music on weekends. On more quiet nights, there are always a number of hard-working husbands out for an
hour at some favorite pub for a few beers. Community
organizations run bowling leagues, and others gather at
fraternal societies. Little adult reading goes on, even
among the women. As with the men, an extremely small
percentage of women are college educated, and almost
none have degrees. These who do are probably teachers,
yet few of Highland's teachers live in the immediate
area. The nearest bookstore is fifteen minutes' drive to
the Cherry Hill shopping mall.

There is a considerable amount of intrafamily visiting,
especially during the months of pleasant weather. A few
play bridge, more play canasta; the men play pinochle. Few
gamble to any degree; there are no large poker games,
for example. Except for church bingo and an occasional
try at a lottery ticket, or, for those who work in Philly,
a random stab at the numbers, there is no talk of it.

In the summer months, the workingman will take his
vacation—usually a family affair—probably a camping
trip to New England or Canada, into the most rural
areas possible, where a man can show his kids a thing or
two about fishing. There is no tradition of culture-
oriented trips to New York or Washington, D.C., to visit
theaters, museums, or historical monuments. As a result,
most local kids spend their entire adolescence without
ever seeing New York or their nation's capital, though
they live within a few hours of both.

For most Blackwoodians, then, each year passes very
much like the last. A new baby is born, a man builds an
addition on his house, buys a new and better car; these
are the changes. When a national election looms before
him every four years, he gets stirred into the controversy
via the news media. He is, more likely than not, a union
man and will vote accordingly. In 1968, Hubert Hum-

phrey had no trouble carrying Camden County, though a considerable percentage (fourteen point five per cent) defected to George Wallace. The local Congressman reelected from this, the First District of New Jersey, was John Hunt, a tough, crew-cut politican with a background in law enforcement. To his admirers, he is a "true patriot, a stand-up guy who fights communism on the national level and takes care of the needs of his community. He's a real man of the people." He is a true hawk on the Vietnam war, critical of any compromise on total victory, believing that such "no-win policies have created a cancerous ulcer that is bleeding America to death." To his critics, "Hunt is an illiterate ex-sheriff (some say he is also an ex-narco agent) who calls pot 'marriage-a-wanna' and considers it a sin to smoke it because 'you're apt to take a lady's stocking, rape her, then choke her to death.' I'll have to admit he's a great campaigner, though. He never stops. They say if you were opening an outhouse, John Hunt would show up to christen it."

However, all the electoral issues appear to be resolved without much passion; it is as though the general flow of Blackwood life would not be affected one way or another regardless of who won any election.

The quality of local politics inevitably suffered through this kind of indifference. Gloucester Township is run by a mayor and town council elected by the people, and their political leadership has been a continued source of cynical abdication among the citizenry. Indeed, what could anyone expect from a mayor whose job pays a mere thousand dollars a year? Commented Chris Parsons, editor and publisher of the weekly Blackwood *Observer:* "We have had a number of terribly inadequate men who became mayors of this township. Smalltown, dirt-cheap, uneducated characters. Some were near-illiterates who could hardly speak a communicable English. One was a garage mechanic and drove a school bus. I don't mean to demean those occupations, but only to show that our politicians . . . weren't the most intelligent or best trained citizens. Many who went into politics did so for the graft, the patronage, the ego gratification. It was, in a way, the apex of their appreciation of what America could do for them, all part of the same system that brought them a certain amount of affluence in the first place. Politics was another game they could play—like bowling, hunting, pinochle, whatever. It was an extension of their social lives. . . .

"There were a few who tried to break in with altruistic goals, to help the community. They are always forced to compromise. It seems to end up, these men make the sacrifice to help the grafters, not the community. The system here is just too tightly organized.

"As a result, there is very little new industry coming in to Gloucester Township, though there is plenty of space and the geography is perfect. It's simply that business people, quite wisely so, thoroughly investigate an area before they take the plunge, and they find that political conditions are too unsettled here.

"To a great extent, the fault lies with the voters, I suppose. The people don't really care. They won't get off their butts and take action. The decent citizens resent the graft, but they end up accepting it as a political reality."

It would follow that civics is a difficult course to teach in the high schools. Inevitably, the kids are the victims who suffer the most, learning their first lessons in cynicism in the homes, followed by hypocrisy in the schools.

"The school board is at the very center of local politics," Parsons commented. "There is no money in the job—at least not in salary—but there's big money in construction of schools. The biggest item in the local budget is school funds."

As a result, the letting of contracts is at the heart of all local political questions. The construction's the thing. It is no accident, then, that building contractors dominate the local political scene, from Mayor Joseph Menna and School Superintendent August Muller on down.

It is perhaps ironic that in such a setting, deficiencies in construction are not uncommon. As young Charlie Kean pointed out, the construction of Highland High School was faulty from its foundation. Neighboring Triton High School was built three feet lower than it ought to have been; after spring rains, water would flood the area, pouring into the front doors. As a result, a moat and drainage ditch had to be built (by the same architect and contractor whose negligence caused the problem) at considerable expense and inconvenience to the citizens (and considerable profit to the builders).

Former Vice President Hubert Humphrey, once a school teacher himself, suggested that the educational process was, indeed, full of contradictions: "What I taught my students about government and politics had little to do with what I learned when I went into government and politics."

All this is, however, a matter of no great consequence in Blackwood. Many are simply amused by it, and the occasional flurry of indignation as expressed by some public-spirited citizen is treated as just another passing phase. The local citizenry is, in the last analysis, essentially content with its lot. Most are enjoying a substantial income, living in far greater affluence than they had been brought up to expect, sharing the mores of their neighbors in what has come to be recognized as the Great Silent Majority of Americans who want to keep things as they are.

Significantly, it is a community without formidable leading citizens. Unlike the old factory towns where the millionaire tycoon controlled the jobs and purse strings of the bulk of its working force, and owned the local newspaper and radio station, there is no central industry in Gloucester Township and no one controls anything. The wealthiest man in town is a native Blackwoodian, a home builder named George Matteo, a classic example of a self-made man, American style.

There is no tradition of high achievement. Aside from Matteo, it would seem that the principal money-maker is Edward C. Gardner, owner of the Gardner Funeral Home on the Black Horse Pike. These men are routine characters in a routine community—reasonably large fish in a reasonably small pool. Incredibly, perhaps, there are no outstanding alumni of Blackwood and environs who have left to become successful in any field: no politicians, no leaders of industry or notable attorneys, no pioneering researchers or doctors, no professional athletes of consequence, no writers, actors, musicians, painters, astronauts, no one anywhere in America who has achieved prominence after an adolescence in these communities. As one of the more whimsical of Craig's friends remarked: "Well, *that* must be a distinction of some kind."

"Of course, there was Walt Whitman, but he came from Camden," said Betty Quemore. "When they built the new bridge to Philly, there was quite a controversy over its naming. When 'Walt Whitman Bridge' was suggested—and he was surely Camden's most famous personality—there were many who objected because, to them, his reputation as a homosexual was more important than his stature as a poet. Fortunately, the latter won out."

Traditions of a community generally tend to be self-perpetuating, generation following generation. However, there are usually those few who rebel against its limitations and plunge into the larger competitions of the world outside. The postwar generation of Blackwood youngsters is just beginning to face this challenge but has yet to come up with a potential winner. "I believe that most of them are really afraid to make the try," said a teacher. "The whole educational system is designed to keep them here. It emphasizes only those values that appear to make life in Blackwood a pleasant life. Everything is oriented toward vocational training with over half the school's energy devoted to the trades. A kid can learn that there are jobs available to him as soon as he graduates, jobs with a decent promise of ten, maybe twelve thousand dollars a year. He can get married quickly and get a home and family going, and maybe, in time, if he has enough brains and ambition, he can get over that twenty-thousand-dollar plateau and move off to Haddonfield. I know boys who went on to college, they could have stretched their legs in other communities, expanded their experiences, but they came back here to settle. The reason? They wanted to do better than their fathers. They wanted to make more money and show them up. It was almost a vengeful thing, not unusual around here, though it isn't stated as such. The fathers are hard-working men and are proud of what they have accomplished. They name their first-born sons after themselves. Almost every family has a 'Junior.'

Kids grow up under the father's dominance, but when they get old enough, they all want to prove they can top him."

This lack of adventurousness is no less prevalent among the girls. Those who avoid the vocational and stay with academic programs struggle to get into a few of the Jersey state colleges (Glassboro, Douglass [at Rutgers]), hoping to become teachers or psychologists. Others take nursing training. Gail Hillias said: "Of the nineteen girls in my senior English class, fourteen were engaged three months before graduation. All to local boys, some in the army, some with local jobs. If you're not married here at nineteen, everybody thinks you're going to be an old maid. And if you settle here after you're married, you'll live here for the rest of your life."

The brightest students at Highland High are traditionally those specializing in math and the sciences, part of the technological explosion in education that erupted after the Soviet launching of sputnik. Every year there are a few like Frank DiGenova who get into the better engineering schools. There are seldom any comparable academic acceptances at the Ivy League schools. Most of the college men settle for Glassboro State or the local Camden County Community College, a few miles down the road from Highland. They will presumably learn to be teachers and return to perpetuate the very educational system that retarded them.

The kids are, in effect, bewildered by this: it is as if they were somehow doomed to some classic American middle level of mediocrity. They graduate from high school and the mystical computer-in-the-sky, having been fed every detail in their history and that of their forebears, tells them that they have absolutely no chance of any consequential success.

The entire process, then, becomes an endless cycle and no one appears to challenge it. Old values are preserved: thrift, hard work, sobriety, honesty, patriotism, reverence, virtuous values they have all been trained to believe in, the values that "made this country the greatest in the world." If they are also uncreative, the risk of departing from them seems small compensation when balanced against the warmth and security of the familiar.

A young man named O'Halloran who had gone to
Triton High School with Bernie Badiali was currently
trying to make his mark in the gruesome world of professional boxing. A short paragraph appeared in the
sports section of the *New York Times* during the winter
of 1970 revealing that O'Halloran had been knocked out
early in a Madison Square Garden prelim. Said Bernie:
"To the best of my knowledge, this makes O'Halloran
our most famous living alumnus."

It took the suicides of Craig Badiali and Joan Fox to
create Blackwood's first nationally known citizens.

11

It was astounding—and dismaying—to the people of Blackwood that the suicides should have attracted such widespread attention. It was one thing to see coverage by the Camden *Courier-Post;* it was quite another to realize that this was a front-page story in major newspapers throughout the country, duly reported on national television news programs as well. There were local citizens who received long distance calls from friends not heard from for many months, hungering for details and explanations. Men who worked in Philadelphia suddenly became the center of their co-workers' interest. The names of Badiali and Fox were prominent even on the front page of *The New York Times.* Indeed, by Friday afternoon, the news was being covered by newspapers in London, Paris, and Rome.

For all its fascination, the suicidal act for peace was not so uncommon a tragedy as to command such attention. The fascination lay principally in the youth of the victims, compounded by their romance and respectability.

Every American war has had its protesters, its conscientious objectors, its dissidents, some of whom, because of religious belief or personal moral code, have opted for jail rather than serve the military or pay taxes in support of it. No war in American history, however, has brought a comparable dissent to that of the current action in Southeast Asia. In 1968, over fifty-three thousand United States servicemen were officially listed as deserters, one hundred and fifty-five thousand more went AWOL. In 1970, that unprecedented figure was topped in the first four months. Thousands more are in jail for draft evasion, and tens of thousands have expatriated themselves to Canada and elsewhere.

It followed that there would also be those who would make the ultimate sacrifice. Since 1965, there were sixteen known suicides that preceded Craig and Joan, an expanding list that began in Washington, D.C., outside the Pentagon itself, when the Quaker, Norman Morrison, doused his clothing with gasoline and set himself on fire—an act that seemed completely alien to the American way. Morrison was in his thirties, a sober, philosophic, religious man with a loving wife and child, and the purity of his motives inevitably touched the sensitivity of millions, aware of their own silence and complicity at the escalation of the Vietnam war. There were others, however, who saw it as an affront to God and the sanctity of human life and condemned it passionately, while their own churches endorsed the war as a preserver of the sanctity of human life. (It was not until June 1969, when the young Czech patriot, Jan Palach, immolated himself in Prague in protest against the Soviet invasion that the Vatican had kind words for a political suicide, having previously denounced similar immolations by the Buddhist monks who protested their own war. It appeared that only suicides with an anticommunist orientation were properly religious.)

A week after Morrison's death, the list began to grow. Roger Laporte, twenty-two, immolated himself in front of the United Nations in New York. In 1966, Mrs. Alice Herz, an eighty-two-year-old refugee from Germany, killed herself in Detroit. In 1967, John Copping, four years a Navy veteran, left this note: "I have carried out my act of immolation as a protest against Johnson's war in Vietnam. The war is, like my final act, a war of frustration." In October a thirty-six-year-old Japanese-American woman, Mrs. Hiroko Hayashi, immolated herself in San Diego, California, and three days later, Mrs. Florence Beaumont, fifty-five, did the same in front of the Federal Building in Los Angeles. Her husband said: "She was a dedicated woman for peace. She couldn't stand to live any longer under this thing." In December, again three days apart, there were two more immolations in the East: Erik Thoem, twenty-seven, and Kenneth D'Elia, the latter at the UN. After the defeat of Senator Eugene McCarthy and the triumph of the pro-Adminstration war forces at the

Democratic convention in 1968, a twenty-two-year-old peaceworker named Minna Gross took an overdose of sleeping pills in New York City. In Kingsport, Tennessee, in July 1969, Claude F. Moyers, Jr., twenty, shot himself in the chest five times rather than be drafted: "I believe it is wrong to kill. . . ." Then, less than three weeks before Moratorium Day, a half-Apache named Leonard Humphrey took his wife, Laurel, and three young children in their family house trailer, ostensibly to visit the Apache sun god in Tucson, Arizona. On the night of September 28, his wife shot him and the children, and then herself. A note was found attributing this horrendous act to the war in Vietnam and the resulting chaos in the world.

Eighteen American suicides for peace in four years—for the most part, widely dispersed in time and geography—men and women of varying age and background and religious (or nonreligious) persuasion. It was not without historical irony that six of the eighteen were immolations in a symbolically religious quest for martyrdom, like Christian martyrs burned at the stake, only to be condemned by the modern Christian church itself.

And it was not without relevance that Craig and Joan were the only teen-agers among them, for therein lay the heart of the nation's concern. Two seventeen-year-olds, lovers, handsome and clean and respectable; it was their normalcy that fascinated everyone. Add two inches to Craig's hair and a long string of beads to Joan's daily attire, and the story would have been buried.

Then too, it was Blackwood's story, for the town itself was at the essence of that normalcy, and now they would find themselves propelled into direct contact with the very viscera of America's anguish for the first time in their collective lives.

12

The living room of the Badiali home was small and cozy, approximately fifteen feet square, large enough for five or six people to sit in comfortably. The kitchen was much larger, having been expanded by breaking into the old dining area and combining the two. As a result, the Badialis liked to gather around the kitchen table for tea and talk, enjoying the easy access to the kettle and the pantry, as well as the telephone that hung on the wall adjacent to the table.

Starting with the tragic Thursday morning of October 16, these two rooms became the setting for an emotional drama that none of its participants would ever forget.

As Bernie recounted it: "It didn't take long after mother heard the news that she was reduced to a pitiful mess. Then everything seemed to happen at once. The police came; they had to make an official report, I guess. Then relatives. Everyone who came in became caught in her hysteria. All my mother's brothers and sisters and cousins (there were dozens of them in the Ivins family), all very close to each other. I made my mother take the tranquilizers and they seemed to help her. Even my dad took them eventually. I think that was the first time in his life he ever took a pill like that.

"Meanwhile, the phone began to ring. It started to ring and it never stopped. I answered it; I thought maybe that was something I could do, to make it easier on my folks. Ring, ring. It was so quick, so sudden, how did everyone know so quickly? Especially the newspaper people. They were calling from all over.

"It was through reporters that we found out about the letters. Twenty-four suicide notes, they said. It added to the horror—the thought that Craig and Joan had written letters and other people had read them. Strangers. Newspapermen. Police. Craig had written and we didn't know what was in them and now the whole world would know about them before we did. It was horrible and infuriating. 'Is it true?' they kept asking. 'Did your brother die as a protest against the war?' I kept saying, I don't want to answer any questions. Please, I didn't know about any letters. Please, leave us alone. Please. But they wanted a statement, they had to have some kind of a statement, they kept saying. It was similar to the way they show the press in the movies, crowded around the door, waving their mikes and cameras and notebooks, pushing and shoving. Horrible. I was afraid that my dad might become violent. He was so broken up, he might have done something, I didn't know what, and it would only have made things worse. It was a fear I would nurse for days. . . .

"I finally decided I would make a statement, thinking someone had to say something to the press. The Foxes refused to talk. Like my parents, they were just too broken up about it, they couldn't communicate with anyone. So I told the reporters and the TV people, I would say something if they agreed to leave us alone. I went to the door and faced all those cameras and all, dozens of people, and I told them that Craig and Joan had died for peace. They asked me a few more questions, nothing I could really answer, I hadn't seen the letters, I didn't know what was in them—I just told them what I knew to be true. And when I left them and came back inside, I didn't know how I had managed to do it.

"I thought about what I had said. I knew that this *was* the way Craig had felt. But how could I be sure it was the reason for his suicide?"

The reporters left, finally, and began a series of visits to the focal points of interest, trying to pick up bits of news and quotes from anyone who would talk. They managed to contact Craig's aunt, Mrs. Mary Ivins, next door on Keystone Avenue: " 'The family is in shock. You can imagine. It's so unbelievable.' Then she wept." Close by the Foxes' home on Theresa Place: " 'Joan was a nice American girl—the kind you would like to have your son

bring home on a date,' said Mrs. Barbara Walter, a
neighbor. 'Why, she's no hippie, not by any means. That's
what makes it seem so impossible.' " At the police station: " 'They're good families, good people,' said Captain
Vincent Mango of the twenty-two-man Gloucester Township Police Force. 'The kids had no records. They weren't
hippies or anything like that. They were just like everybody else. We're confused. Why did they do it?' " At the
morgue in Pennsauken: "Dr. Louis Reigert, the Camden
County medical examiner, read the notes but had nothing
to say."

Thom Akeman of the Camden *Courier-Post* made all
these rounds, marking time until three o'clock when he
could return to the Highland Regional High School,
where the story would inevitably be expanded. As the
wire services and radio reports introduced the peace-
suicide headline throughout the country, there was an
increasing demand for follow-up coverage. Details.
Everyone wanted details. Who were these kids? What
was the nature of their lives? And why, *really*, did they
do it?

Shortly before two in the afternoon, the police got
through to the Badiali home, requesting that a member
of the family come to the morgue to identify the body.
It was, of course, Bernie, Jr., who would have to submit
to this. "I hung up the phone thinking it was a terrible
prospect and I didn't know if I could go through with it.
Then I thought, maybe, just maybe, it wasn't really
Craig. Maybe there had been a mistake. There just might
have been a mistake. . . ."

A police car came to pick him up, and he saw Andrew
Fox, Jr., in the rear seat. That, too, jarred him, this first
confrontation of the two families since the unfolding of
the tragedy, and he could not help but wonder what had
been brewing in the minds of the Foxes.

"All the way over to Pennsauken, the police officer
who was driving us kept talking about the goddam hippies, blaming them for somehow causing all this to happen, telling how he'd like to kill them, repeating that
over and over, how he'd like to kill all the hippies. It
was a horrible thing to have to listen to. I just sat there

hoping he would shut up, or maybe Andy would say something to him; after all, they were policemen together. Finally, he did shut up, and we rode in silence for a while. Then Andy turned to me—I could feel that he'd been thinking a long time about what he was going to say —and he said that he hoped that neither of our families would blame the other for any of this. I said, no, I hoped not too. But somehow, it began to eat away at me that the Foxes had been thinking about this already. Had they blamed Craig for bringing it about? It was a moment when you can't feel any hostility, you can only feel compassion. I felt close to Andy. The whole thought of blame was too depressing to contemplate. I just felt where it came from and why. I could even understand how they might think that their daughter could not have possibly dreamed up such a crazy sick thing as suicide, that it must have been Craig. But when I thought of them saying that to each other, I found myself thinking just the opposite, that it must have been Joan who initiated it.

"God, it was a terrible car ride."

The arrival at the medical examiner's office in Pennsauken was infinitely worse. "We walked into Dr. Reigert's place, and the first sound I heard was the World Series on the radio. Mr. Daley was there, all dressed up in a sharkskin suit. He was so young and clean-cut, you wouldn't think he'd be the type to be a coroner. He explained as how they had the bodies inside and that it might be best if he took us in one at a time. Well, Andy went first, I don't know why, it just happened that way. I sat down and waited, wondering whether I would have wanted to go first or not. I just sat there, it seemed like an hour, and I knew I would know everything when he came out, that if it wasn't Joan he'd been looking at, then it wouldn't be Craig either. Finally, when he came out, he was crying. Not just red-eyed and teary, he was really crying with his hand up in front of his eyes. And like a fool—God, I felt like a fool—I asked him if it was Joan.

"Then they took me inside and led me to the window, the big glass window that kept you from the body and maybe the smell, I don't know. They had a body laid out there on the slab, and for an instant, just for an instant, I thought there was still hope that it might not be.

"It was an appalling sight. Discolored. Reddish. It was horrible. Somehow, I kept my composure. I think, after seeing my mother break down, I'd seen the worst. There couldn't be anything worse than that. The way I felt, I was standing in front of my brother, and all I could think of was what this was doing to my mother. I don't think that if someone had gone and shot my wife I could have been more broken up than when I had seen my mother that moment in the living room when she first heard the news."

Bernie and Andy returned to the squad car for the trip back home. This time in total silence. To Bernie, the specter of a second confrontation suddenly loomed in his consciousness, as though his family were sitting there waiting for him with that same desperate last-ditch anticipation of a miracle that he had sensed himself a few moments before. He thought perhaps he should have called to tell them, to relieve them of any new layer of suspense. But now it was too late for that. He would have to walk inside and they would be staring at him—the way he had stared at Andy—and then what? He would have to tell them all with his eyes and his tears and it would begin all over again.

But when he drove onto Keystone Avenue, a formidable barrier of the press and TV was there to cut him down and he cringed in the rear of the car, suddenly completely unable to move, and all he could think of was how quickly he had come to hate them, the whole lot of them, the good ones, the nice ones, and the others, all lumped together in one ugly fraternity of enemies.

They spotted him, of course, and he moved to get free of the entrapment of the car, to get himself inside his house as rapidly as possible. He was conscious of cameras again, and the same steady spate of questions. "Why?" "Why?" in a dozen different forms, so that he could no longer make sense of it. They were blocking his way to the door, maybe eight or ten of them, and finally he was stopped completely.

"Please . . . please . . ." he stammered. "I'll talk to

you all later. I'll make a statement for the family. I promise. I promise. . . ."

So they let him through, and he shut the door quietly behind him. The living room was empty, and that helped him. Everyone would be in the kitchen, then. Yes, he could hear them through the alcove a few dozen feet away.

"I was all worn out. I thought it was only about three o'clock and I could hardly stand any more of it. I thought now I was going to have to go in there and they would all look up at me and God knows what would begin again. . . .

"They were sitting around the kitchen table, maybe six or seven, uncles and aunts with my folks. They were drinking coffee and no one was crying any more. I couldn't believe it. They barely looked at me as I came in, not even my mother. She just got up from the table and poured me a cup of coffee, and I pulled over a chair and sat down with them. They weren't even talking about Craig. They were just chatting, telling random things like they might on a normal Sunday afternoon with nothing better to do. It didn't seem real. Nothing seemed real. It was so weird, I thought maybe I had gone crazy.

"Then after a while I noticed that no one was looking at anyone else."

13

Gail Hillias (who had dreamed so portentously) spent the morning in bed, nursing herself through the discomfort of a cold. She read for a while, slept when she could, and tried to enjoy the luxury of being alone in the quiet house. Her father was a truck driver, her older sister was at work, her younger brother was at school, and her mother, who worked in an elementary school cafeteria, would not be home until afternoon. Gail was a bright girl, talented and serious-minded, constantly probing for answers to all the big questions. She felt a strong religious tie, having been brought up in the Greek Orthodox Church. Indeed, she found some difficulty dealing with others who did not share her faith in God. Yet her mind was malleable and she kept fumbling for the meaning and purposes of life on a level she felt neither her parents nor teachers could give her.

It was early in the afternoon that she turned on her radio, only half-listening as she moved through the house, hearing snatches of news that curled their way into her slightly feverish consciousness. "Craig Badiali . . . Joan Fox . . . dead . . . a car . . ." For a moment, she could not separate the sound from her subconscious, as if the radio were an intrusion on the memory of a dream not quite ended.

And when it sank in as "real," she rushed to the telephone, frightened, yet not knowing exactly whom to call. She dialed Joan's number, and felt relieved at the busy signal. She dialed Craig's, but hung up before it had a chance to ring. She listened to the radio with total concentration, waiting for the news to repeat itself, but knew the folly of that. She dressed herself in defiance of her illness, then hurried toward the only place where she could find surcease: Highland Regional High School. On the way, she would pass Joan's house, barely two blocks away.

Gail went by from a distance of less than two hundred yards where Theresa Place curved gently away from South Drive. She saw the cars parked all around it, at least seven or eight, right out in front, and people standing around. It frightened her from coming closer, knowing that all her worst fears were true, that she should have known from her foreboding dream . . . and suddenly sensing how terrifying was the essence of it, she hurried as fast as she could down Church Street toward school.

The last school period had not yet finished, but there were always some students and teachers in the halls, especially around the administration offices. "I guess I expected to see troubled people and a lot of tears, but everything was normal. Nobody seemed to know anything at all!"

It was true: the principal had succeeded in keeping the tragic news completely buried throughout the school day, a problem simplified by school regulations that prohibited students from leaving the grounds even at lunch hour (during which they might have heard it on the radio). Incredible though it must have seemed to Gail, no news had actually penetrated this fortress. There was at least one radio within its walls, in the manual arts shop in the basement, but no reports had spread through the student body.

As a result, Gail became even more bewildered by the garbled story she thought she had heard at home, and it wasn't until others began spreading the true story that the news began to make sense to her.

Even then, after the three o'clock bell, there was no official announcement to the students, though the P.A. system was readily available for such purposes and was used daily. The principal, Mrs. Forneron, assembled the faculty in the library on the main floor and made the announcement to them. Carleton Sherwood, reporter on the weekly Blackwood *Observer,* and other members of the press were there—including Thom Akeman and Andrea Knox of the Camden *Courier-Post*—and those teachers who wished to comment were asked to do so.

"Why?" came the question, over and over. "Why did they do it?"

Mrs. Diane Wagner immediately broke into tears and fled the building. Others who knew one or both of the kids were completely shocked. It was, in effect, incomprehensible to any of them. "Joan was wonderfully full of life, outgoing and animated," said Mrs. Ann Walsh, the librarian. "They gave no signs of being involved in teen-age problems like drinking and narcotics," said athletic director, James Ackert. "They were wholesome —the kind we're proud of," he added, making mention of the fact that Joan was, indeed, an outstanding cheerleader as well as a member of the hockey team. Mrs. Forneron reported that, though she had no knowledge of any of their political or religious views, they had made no attempt to organize any sort of antiwar activity within the school. Craig and Joan were, it was repeatedly pointed out, average, pleasant, exuberant kids, the last people one might expect capable of such an aberrated act.

In the halls, in gathering places around individual lockers, and outside the administration offices there were pockets of students who were unable to move out of the building. By this time, Gail Hillias had completely broken down in tears. Debbie Gliick was choked up, unable to speak. Another friend of Joan's, Ginny Kamulda, younger and less sophisticated, was on her way to Color Guard practice with the band when she heard. She couldn't understand it. She heard several kids laughing about it and simply assumed it was some sort of sour joke, that perhaps everyone was teasing her because she was so friendly with Joan. But then the truth sank in, the cold, horrid truth; she could not cope with it. She disintegrated in tears, and the others stopped laughing. Ginny did not continue with band practice.

Many remained in the halls for a long time, and one could hear the muted sound of sobbing and whispered voices wherever one passed. Stanley Pietrowksi grieved and raged at the death of his friend, knowing too little and caring too much to know against whom his rage might be directed. He saw dozens of little girls crying, seeking to share the mutual anguish, and not even knowing them, could not trust their grief and rejected the show of it. Mark Bunzell, the sophomore who had looked up to Craig as one might revere a big brother, heard the news from a boy who was a stranger to him, coldly, "like someone telling me the World Series score." He had had no inkling of it, hadn't even known that Craig was not in school on that day.

When the press came out of the faculty meeting, they sought the students who were closest to the couple, but most of them were not available for comment. As Stanley put it: "I needed to talk about it, but not to a stranger and not for newspapers. Hell, I didn't know anything about what had happened. Like those letters. Right off, we heard there were letters, but what was in them and who did they write them to? I wanted to know about those letters."

Bill Billhardt, Jr., was more cooperative. "Craig was such a great kid," he told a reporter. "He took time to understand people. He just wished everyone could live in harmony. He really tried."

Others said much the same about Joan. "I wouldn't feel right about getting my name in the paper because of her death," said a senior boy. "She was sincere, you know. She didn't say what she didn't believe. She just wanted to be a real person."

Reporters roamed through the halls, questioning kids at random. Casual acquaintances said they were nice, happy-go-lucky, all-around neat people, friendly, yes, above all, friendly. At least thirty said they hadn't the slightest idea why they had done this thing, not understanding the peace message. If any others thought they knew, no one came forward to say. It was reported that Joan had signed her classmates' yearbooks in the previous spring with a peace symbol under her name, but neither she nor Craig was thought of as a "radical." They belonged to no peace organizations, and it was explained that there were no such organizations around Blackwood to which they might have belonged.

A senior girl, Chris Henderson, had seen a lot of Craig over the years. "We had talked about those other protest suicides, like the monks in Saigon and the student in

Czechoslovakia who had burned themselves to death. Craig had said that he didn't know what they thought they were proving, that it was just more dead persons."

Outside, in the parking area adjacent to the school, Ed Bonnet added his confusion to the others. "A year ago, on Veterans' Day, November 11, they marched with me to Camden in support of the soldiers in Vietnam. It was in all the papers. About six months ago, they both dropped out of the organization; they just stopped coming. But I don't understand this. Craig was a mild and gentle person. I would never guess he would do a thing like this."

It was the gist of all the newspaper reports. The Philadelphia *Daily News* reporter heard a classmate make note that "Joan reminded me of Julie Nixon—the way she wore her hair and all."

It was Bill Billhardt, Jr., who wrapped it all up through his gathering tears: "I just feel that nothing was gained by it."

14

Around three o'clock that Thursday afternoon, eighteen-year-old Charlie Kean, a recent graduate of Highland High School, was waiting at the Philadelphia bus terminal to board a bus to New York. He had most of his possessions with him: a suitcase full of clothes, his electric guitar, seventy-odd dollars cash. He was leaving, literally, to seek his fortune as a rock musician. Too nervous to sit, he stood around trying to enjoy the age-old pastime of looking at people, all sorts of people; but in time, the process only served to feed his own anxieties.

Charlie was a slight, good-looking, dark-haired boy, currently sporting a mustache and goatee in keeping with the style of his intended profession. If he was a troubled boy with a confused history, he was also extremely bright and everyone considered his potential far greater than his performance. "I'm slow. I'm slow at everything. I'm the type who takes a long time to trust anyone or anything. I just can't make it with people very easily." It was this quality that left him uneasy at his pending adventures in New York, and he was musing about it when, like a clap of thunder, he heard the sound of his name called over the public address system. "Charles Kean, please come to the information counter. Charles Kean . . ."

"It was my sister, and all she kept saying was that something terrible had happened and I should come right back home. I kept asking her, 'What? What?' and finally she told me. Oh my God, I thought, and I started to cry even before I could hang up the phone. In my whole life, one guy had showed me how it was to be a friend, and now he was dead."

"Steve Karras" was not his real name. He was a boy who had much to say, but did not wish his name used for fear of embarrassing others (especially his parents) or creating problems for himself with the authorities. He was a senior at Highland, a classmate of the two suicides, and had been friendly with Craig over the years, "but most especially in the last year or so." Like most other Blackwoodians, his family had moved into the area out of the disquiet of life in Philadelphia during the prospering postwar years (his father was a skilled technician, currently working at a subcontract plant with the aerospace program) and Steve had grown up in a pleasant suburban home on a quarter-acre plot. He was bright, conservative, healthy, and popular with both students and teachers. He did not think of himself as troubled, certainly not in any fundamental way.

"We were standing around in the halls the way you do when you don't know what else you're supposed to do. You feel sort of stupid, I guess. The reporters—there must have been a dozen of them—were asking the same question of everyone: 'Why?' 'Why?' One of them came up to me, said he'd heard that I was a friend of Craig's. 'Why did they do it?' he asked.

"I thought of how I couldn't possibly answer that, the whole thing seemed so God-awful crazy, I couldn't think straight. I looked at the man, he was polite and all, but he must've been strange himself to think *anyone* could answer a thing like that. I just couldn't say anything.

" 'Suicides?'

"It didn't make sense to me at all.

"I couldn't even say that. I just had to get away from there before I broke into tears. I had to get away from school. I had to get away from everyone. All these kids bawling in the halls, dozens of kids, I guess maybe it was infectious, the impact the news had on everyone. Or maybe it was considered the thing to do. Whatever. I didn't want to talk to anyone, even friends. It was interesting, the different kinds of friends they had. There were so many different types. From the straight kids like myself, Mark Bunzell, Bill Billhardt, John Millet, Tom Bye—all old friends of Craig's—to the way-out kids like Stanley, Liz Quemore, Desi. I mean, we were worlds apart but we had this one thing in common. My parents, they could never understand that. Especially my father. They'd hear about Desi or Stanley and they couldn't understand what I'd be doing even talking to them. I couldn't explain it, really. Though we never agreed on much, I liked them and they seemed to like me, and we got along okay. That was what was so great about Craig and Joan: they brought different people together.

"I wanted to be alone, and when I got home, I didn't want to say anything to my mother, so I just went into my room and shut the door. I lay down on my bed and stared up at the ceiling for a while, and I thought about them, trying to let the fact of their being dead sink in. But it just didn't seem possible. 'They're dead!' I said it out loud. 'Dead! Dead!' I just couldn't picture it. I must have said it a hundred times and tried to think about why they did it, but it didn't make sense. I thought of Craig —not that he was always bubbling with joy—and the picture of him doing this suddenly grabbed me and tore me apart. I began to cry in a way I hadn't cried since I was a kid. It wasn't the way the tears came out, it was the feeling in my stomach. It was an agony that hurt physically as well as emotionally. I don't know how long I cried, maybe an hour or so. I'd stop for a while, and then I'd think about them and it would start up all over again. I thought, well, okay, I'd cry myself out, at least I thought that's what happens. But there seemed to be no end to it, I had an unlimited supply and it kept washing out of me.

"The phone rang a few times in the other room, and once my mother knocked on the door, and when I didn't answer, she left me alone. My mother, she's great, she kept my kid brothers away from me too, and I just stayed there until it was dark.

"My father was home by then, and he didn't say anything. He just slapped me on the butt with the back of his hand, just to let me know he was there if I wanted him. We were at the dinner table when the news came on the TV from Philly. It was the first time I'd heard it mentioned over the air, but none of us stopped eating, pretending that nothing had happened, I guess, because it would have been too obvious if someone had gotten up and turned it off. I didn't get upset. In fact, I listened to it all, all that business about how no one could understand why it had happened.

"My father stopped eating and cleared his throat, but he didn't say anything. Not at first. He glanced at my mother the way parents do—I could tell they'd been talking about it—and then he spoke up.

" 'Well, they say they must have been taking something. . . .'

"For a moment it didn't register, and when it did, I said the word he didn't say: 'Drugs?' I felt rotten. Somehow it seemed like a very insulting thing.

" 'No,' I said, 'that couldn't be true.'

" 'How do you know?' he asked. 'Some of those friends they had. You, yourself told me . . .'

"It was his tone that got to me now, like he'd practically made up his mind already. 'I know that's not so, that's all,' I said.

" 'I heard they went to the Moratorium,' he said, like it went with the drugs.

"I didn't say anything after that, and neither did he. But I couldn't sit there any longer. I rose from the table and excused myself. I had to get out of the house. I was really confused now."

Mark Bunzell was another who went home and cried. "Eventually, I went for a walk the way you do when you can't sit still; it's easier to think about things when you're moving. I ended up at a girl's house, a friend, where I could talk about it. I called home to tell my father that I was okay, so he wouldn't think I'd do something foolish. It's weird how that thought comes into your mind: you have no intention of doing anything like that at all but you think everyone is afraid that somebody might.

"I talked about the suicides, but it didn't help, the way I was feeling. It seemed like such a waste, a terrible waste. I didn't like the feeling I had. I really couldn't see what they were trying to prove."

Mark's mother was president of the Gloucester Township chapter of the PTA. On that day, they were in convention in Atlantic City. "Late that afternoon, we were all lining up for the Grand March just before the banquet when someone mentioned that there'd been a double suicide in my neck of the woods. They'd heard it on the radio, they said. They didn't remember who it was, but you could immediately hear the reactions: 'Hippies . . . the girl must've been pregnant . . . they were on dope . . .' I didn't know quite what to say since I didn't know who they were talking about. Then, when I heard, I knew they were wrong. I told them, no, it wasn't that way. But when they asked me why, I really couldn't answer."

15

Among many of the couple's friends, there was a need to come together. There were no invitations, no phone calls that initiated it—a number of kids simply began to drift toward a central place: the Quemore house. It was not without precedent. The bright red reconverted barn just off the old Peanut Line railroad had always been a meeting place for kids, its large barnlike room downstairs having been decorated for a rendezvous they'd named "The Psychedelic Palace."

The Quemores were a large family of three sons, a daughter, and Liz, the resident niece. The boys were superb athletes, from the oldest, Jim, now a teacher in the elementary school system, to sixteen-year-old Curt, a junior at Highland. The seventeen-year-old daughter, Chaneth, a senior at Highland, was on the cheerleader squad with Joan. The home was rich with books and phonograph records (including hundreds of old 78s and Chicago jazz singles from the 1930s). In this house, there was an endless flow of dialogue and discussion and controversy, together with a variety of musical sounds, and dozens of kids who sought a kind of stimulation not otherwise found in the community.

Then too, they were political people, openly active and outspoken liberals. They had marched in civil rights demonstrations, locally and in Washington, D.C. They had demonstrated for peace in opposition to the war in Vietnam. They had protested the suffocating rigidities of local politics and were in the forefront of school groups, youth groups, community action groups, wherever a needy cause presented itself. All this had created an air of eccentricity about them, yet even those who found their ideas too controversial for comfort could not fault their individual conduct. The kids were always neat, bright, respectful, talented. They were better than average students, fine athletes, musical, spirited, good-looking, and wholesome. One could almost suspect that if they were disliked it was largely out of envy.

On this Thursday afternoon, members of the family drifted home independently of each other, as was customary, from an assortment of activities immediately suspended, each of them deeply affected by the suicides in some personal way. Chan, the cheerleader, had shared that activity with Joan and became friendly with her over the two years of this mutual effort. Chan had gone to cheerleader practice at three o'clock and only then learned of the tragedy. "What hit me so hard was that most of the others had heard of it but didn't see why they shouldn't go right on with practice, as if nothing had happened."

Liz came home stunned. She curled her legs under her on the living-room sofa and smoked cigarettes, one after another.

Then others began to gather, dozens of them. First among them was Stanley, a frequent visitor on both the best and worst of days. The Quemores' home was Stanley's emotional *pied-à-terre;* if his parents found this less than satisfying, they knew better than to be contentious about it, for Stanley was a boy who insisted on going his own way, seeking friendships and gratifications wherever he could, no matter what the hour or the geography.

Another sure bet to arrive was Desi Worland, desperately in need of kinship now, forced to confront another tragic chapter in a life that seemed all too replete with them.

Many came, from all over town. The straight kids were among them, some who had never been to the Quemores' before. They came because they sensed that something important had happened to them all; they wanted to sit around and talk about it, to thrash it out, to see what, if anything, might be done about it.

They talked through the afternoon, and others came in the evening until it was finally decided that they would hold a memorial candlelight march on the following Wednesday, six days hence. It would start at Highland

Regional High School and proceed down Church Street, across the Black Horse Pike to the field behind the Quemore house, where a ceremony would take place. They formed committees to organize each aspect of it; to get a permit from the police; to meet with the mayor (Joseph Menna) to clear details with him; to consult with the families of the couple; to buy candles for everyone; to have a sympathetic minister to lead them; to arrange for a proper and respectful ceremony.

That evening, other friends of the two gathered at Gail Hillias's house: Bob Brower, Chris Henderson, Debbie Gliick among them. There were those who had met at the Quemores' earlier and had not found satisfaction in that strange ambiance. ("Too far out for me," commented Bob Brower. "All that sitting around on the floor and singing folk songs and staring at a candle . . .") This group did not feel the need for demonstration, nor did they believe it was necessary or desirable to commemorate the suicides. Most of them were frightened by the horror of the act, and for all their grief and affection for the two, they could neither condone nor sympathize with its purpose. Gail was the most articulate: "I think they did this because they could not find anything they could do to make life worthwhile for themselves. They wanted the best possible world, but they wouldn't do anything in a struggle to achieve it. They wanted to accomplish something the easy way. I don't really believe they knew what they were doing when they did it. They chose their timing very well; they died on the Moratorium Day so they could make a big thing of their deaths, but I think they died in vain. It was a waste. I also think it's a silly thing to sit around and think up ways to make sense out of it."

Debbie Gliick agreed that it would all end up a waste. "They should not have done this. They should have stayed alive and fought for what they believed."

"I don't see where they are going to change anyone's mind, even about the war," said Chris Henderson.

"It won't accomplish anything," said Bob Brower. "With Craig, I didn't know he felt so strongly about the war. At least he never talked about it with me."

They read some of Joan's poetry, and grieved at its bittersweet loveliness:

Last night
I remembered winter
I remembered ice like sparkling jewels on a tree
I remembered the snow that blew across
    my window in the wind
And I thought, if it just keeps on blowing,
    where will it ever fall?
This morning,
The summer sun bounced off a car window
And burned my eyes.
The world was so hot
I was afraid to touch anything,
Even myself.
Then I thought, how frightening it was,
The way things can change.

I saw a little boy today
He wasn't more than three,
He cocked his head and passed me by
Pretending he was seven.
I saw a little girl today
She looked a lot like me,
She danced around the living room
Pretending it was heaven.

I wish I could hold a thought in my mind
As I would a rose bud,
Then I could nurse it
Until it opens up
And becomes a beautiful thing.

Craig's closest friend during the previous year, Frank DiGenova, was at Rensselaer Polytechnic Institute at Troy, New York, beginning a difficult adjustment to the rigors and disciplines of freshman year. ". . . What a funny world," Frank had written in Craig's high school yearbook in the previous spring. "And how confused we are about so much, me anyway. There's not a whole lot I'm sure of in this world. I love Ann very very much.

And I know that you are a very good person. Quite the kind of person I wish I were. . . ." Now, five months later, he was several hundred miles away from home and family, from Ann Schramm (who was at Douglass College in New Jersey), lonely and determined in a competitive struggle that was far more demanding than he had ever imagined.

The last thing he needed in this chilling unfriendly autumn was that evening call from his home with the news of Craig's death.

He, too, could only begin to speculate on the why of it all, wondering how close he himself had come to such an end as he prepared for the long trip home for the funeral.

On that same day, the Blackwood *Observer*, published on Thursdays (too late to include news of the suicides), was being delivered throughout Gloucester Township. Its lead editorial dealt with the impact of the previous day's Moratorium demonstrations. It was titled: "A CAUSE FOR NATIONAL MOURNING."

The specter of Americans across the nation in a mass demonstration in support of North Vietnam is but one example of the creeping madness that became evident in our country five years ago.

It was only a year or so earlier that Soviet Premier Khrushchev labeled us a decandent nation that would wither from within and drop like a ripe plum into the hands of the Communist world.

At the time, his statements seemed ridiculous since evidence of decadence was hard to find.

Little did we know then what was to come.

Today incomprehensible decadence is rampant all around us. Our news media are having a Roman holiday exploiting riots, violent protest movements, and demonstrations for all manner of grievances as though the normal democratic processes were dead.

We have seen colleges encourage our children to

experiment with dope and national TV time given to mentally sick advocates of LSD. We have seen State Senators support college professors who admit they are Communists teaching our children the philosophies of our enemies.

We have seen our courts free admitted murderers to roam the streets for new victims and justice delayed three years or more while criminals go free on bail to further infect society.

We have seen countless acts of treason against our country actually applauded by some of our elected public officials and members of the clergy.

Can this be anything but madness?

The great paradox of all this is that here in our own community one is hard put to find anyone who is even remotely sympathetic to any of this madness. So what is the answer? Is less than 1% of the population dictating our moral standards and proscribing our way of life? . . . .

The Camden *Courier-Post* had a daily columnist, Stephen Allen, a gentle, poetic young man who wrote with deep feeling and occasional anger, and as a result, became a controversial figure to many thousands of his daily readers.

On the day the suicides were discovered, Allen came to Blackwood. He would write what he saw and heard, and he would return on successive days. On that Thursday, he went to Bee's Lane and saw the deep red and gold leaves that had fallen on the pale blue car and the young bodies within it, and suffered a foreboding that the winter would be a barren one in this community. He spoke to an elderly couple on Keystone Avenue, a few doors away from the Badialis' house; they were tuned to the World Series on television, and when they heard about Craig, they, too, could not comprehend it. "He was a quiet boy. I don't believe I ever said two words to him except to say hello. He was just a nice normal boy. The whole family was nice. His father was a career man in the Air Force, and he thought the world of those two boys." That was the way it went, Allen saw. It had been the same at Glassboro the day before when a buzz went through the crowd: "The Mets are up, 3 to 1!" and all around them the others were singing: "All we are saying is give peace a chance . . ."

In the Editor's Mail Bag, on the page directly behind Stephen Allen's column, there was a letter from "a deeply concerned loyal American" who likened the Moratorium demonstrations to the appeasement of Neville Chamberlain at Munich in 1938. "Like it or not, Vietnam is our frontier. Instead, we give aid and comfort to the enemy by our division. God only knows to what extent the do-gooders in our country have prolonged the war and cost so many American lives they claim to be concerned about."

The Philadelphia *Daily News* polled the local public as to its feelings about the Moratorium. Of the 78.6 per cent of the people who said they knew about it:

57.4 per cent thought it was an over-all bad idea.
31.7 per cent thought it was an over-all good idea.
10.9 per cent had no opinion.

Asked whether they believed President Nixon was doing all he could to settle the war in Vietnam:

68.5 per cent said yes.
29 per cent said no.
10.6 per cent had no opinion.

There was no Inquiring Reporter along the Black Horse Pike as to local reactions on the twin suicides. No one took a poll on it. The people themselves were doing the asking. What had happened? Why did they do it? In the taverns and gathering places that Thursday evening, there was frequent mention of it. "Crazy mixed-up kids . . . It's gotta be tough on the parents, that's for sure. . . . You get the real story, the inside story they'll sure as hell cover up, and I'll tell you this: there's dope involved!"

At the old Chew's Landing Hotel Tavern, one man tried to sum it up over a glass of beer. "They wanted peace? Well, they got peace."

16

The Badiali family slept fitfully that first night of bereavement in spite of their total exhaustion and the assistance of tranquilizers. Said Bernie: "When you wake up, a small part of you wonders if what had happened had just been a terrible dream. And when you see that it wasn't, you shudder at the prospects of facing your grief again. . . . In the kitchen, I had only to look at my mother and I thought, how in the world was she going to live through this. I got so I thought that if Craig could have known the way this would hit us, he never would have done it. He just wouldn't. . . ."

Then, early Friday morning, the police brought over a letter.

"I looked at the envelope, that same pale blue airmail paper and I remembered it right away. I remembered seeing him at his desk, two nights ago. I had not even wondered what he was doing with that paper then. It just never entered my mind."

It was addressed to his mother and father, but it had already been slit open with a sharp instrument. Dolly Badiali took it, sitting down, fingering the envelope for a second or two; there was something terribly disturbing about someone else having read it first. A letter. A boy's last letter to his parents—and they didn't even leave that alone.

It was a short note. Craig had known exactly what he'd wanted to say and he'd written it rapidly. The gist of it was he loved his mother and father deeply and he didn't want them to think that they were to blame. ". . . It's not your fault. This is something I felt I had to do." He wrote that he wanted to be cremated. He didn't want a funeral. He hated the thought of a lot of people standing around before a ceremony, looking at his corpse embalmed in a casket. (As Bernie put it: "I remembered him speaking of this some time ago. He had gone to a funeral and he said how it was horrible to see a thing like that.") He wrote that he was sorry he had to do this. Deeply sorry.

Two pages. A moment to read, and that was it.

Seventeen years of a son's life, and it had come to this. Dolly Badiali folded the two blue pages and put them back in the envelope. The letter was Craig, yes; the sweetness and love was there in those few lines. But all that was Craig's sadness and loneliness and distress —what he wanted to say to everyone, the why of it all— that wasn't there. It seemed so pitifully inadequate. The mother and father sat at the table and the letter lay there in front of them, and they were left to suffer not only their grief, but the devastating sense of their own inadequacy.

"I didn't know what was happening to all those letters," Bernie lamented. "There was supposed to be a pile of them and there was only this one to show for it. It was Friday, the day after, the papers were full of stories about them. They even printed the 'Why?' letter, an actual photograph of Craig's writing, and there was a picture of the coroner, Thomas Daley, holding the others, saying that he had read them all. I couldn't get over that. Not only did he read them, he'd told the press about them. What right had he to do that?"

Yet nothing was said about this in the Badiali household, for grief hung too heavily on them to cope with any such tangential matters. They neither knew nor bothered to find out who had them or what was being done with them.

Later in the day, Mrs. Fox called, having been given their letter from Joan. She wanted to see the Badialis, to share the content of their messages, if possible, especially since there were specific instructions about the burials.

It was another tortured confrontation, this anguish of mothers with unanswerable doubts, with solicitude inevitably tinged with ambivalences so delicately balanced, all those grim, gnawing doubts that could never be stated. My daughter, your son—why did this happen? It was there between them, a festering pain of guilt versus recrimination. Yes, who was to blame? They both knew it would never be spoken, and they regarded each other with whatever compassion they could generate, relative strangers that they were, resisting this hostile thing that hung over them, neither of them wanting it, hating it, hating themselves for sensing it. Strangers, yes, and that, too, was a tragic thing. Your daughter, my son . . . what had they done to each other, what was this thing between them that brought them to their deaths?

They exchanged letters and each wondered at the emotion of the other. "Joan's letter was similar to Craig's," Bernie said. "You could tell how they must have talked about it. Joan wrote more deeply, though. Her letter was longer, much better written. She, too, told her folks that it wasn't their fault. They wanted to be martyrs. She used that word. She did not think it was a cowardly act, or that they were copping out. She said she believed deeply in what they were doing."

The two mothers embraced in parting, as close together as they would ever come in this period of their mutual grieving. And when they separated, they were left with their failures and a residue of unanswered questions that would never be otherwise.

So much of the tragedy was there in that meeting. It was, perhaps, inescapable. There was so much to say and nothing could be said. How could any of it possibly be spoken, for the words would have torn holes in them. Was it not better to say nothing? Two letters were all they had left, read and reread and now shared, and there was nothing else to turn to.

From the two families there would be only resignation and silence.

Friday quickly became a grotesque extension of Thursday's distress. "It was like being clubbed all over again . . . there seemed to be no end to it." The family gathered again and sat around the grieving mother as Bernie faced the constantly ringing telephone and relentless rapping on the door. There were details to be faced now and planning to be done. Was there to be a cremation as Craig had requested? Was the funeral to be avoided? It was immediately clear that this would be no simple problem, regardless of Craig's wishes, for there were too many ramifications and pressures, no matter which course they decided to take.

Bernie and his father discussed it, "trying as hard as we could to think it through clearly. The trouble was, every thought suggested something that set you off and the tears start flowing and swallow you up."

A funeral or no? Cremation or no?

What, these two asked each other, was best for the mother? And if, as a result, the answer ran counter to Craig's wishes, what should take precedence? The needs of the living or the requests of the dead?

Meanwhile, members of the press and of television continued to be an intrusion. The two families could hardly make a move without an irritating awareness of their presence. NBC-TV news saw a major story in the tragedy and sent a documentary team rushing down to Blackwood (professional technicians, writers, directors, cameramen) to film the funerals and piece together whatever meanings they could derive from a series of interviews; to provincial Blackwoodians, it seemed like an invasion of a foreign and hostile force. "I would not say that we were especially well-received," quipped one of its writer-producers, Rafael Abramovitz.

"At the time, we didn't care about the news people and their problems," said Bernie. "Craig had died. It was a time of suffering and nothing else mattered."

It was a time when Bernie, for one, began to ponder the why of it all, and like any sensitive young man, attributed to himself a heavy load of the guilt. Sins of omission and sins of commission; sins that dated back to early childhood. Rivalries and animosities he could not help but relive, inevitably magnifying his involvement, especially that which might have been destructive to Craig's ego.

"Though the initial shock was really pretty terrible, what follows is just as horrible, a gut-wrenching reaction that drains you over and over. In time, you start coming down. A numbness and fatigue sets in. That scream of agony dwindles to a low steady moan. Then you begin to think, your mind begins to play with it, to nurse it, to remember things, and the whole business gets to be really frightening.

"Sure, it was the suicide business. A death is one thing. You can accept that because the chances are that you cannot help it. It just happens. But suicide is personal. Every psychiatrist will tell you that. A boy commits suicide and his family immediately thinks about how much they are at fault—no matter how strongly he tries to convince them otherwise. Like they say, it's a hostile act and you don't have to know much psychology to know exactly what that means.

"I knew how everyone was going to feel guilty. You find a dozen reasons to blame yourself. You could have done this or you shouldn't have done that. You can't help yourself. The guilt takes over. Then I figured the whole thing out. It was really my fault. I had been the apple of my father's eye. When he came home from the service, I stole all the glory in the family. Craig had been a fat young kid, ashamed of his body. I was lean and strong and athletic, just the way my dad would want a son to be. Dad was proud of me. He thought what Craig enjoyed doing, the nonathletic stuff, was almost sissy-like. Craig must have felt he wasn't really loved, but I kept craving for more of it, especially from Dad. I could never get enough of it. It was always me, not Craig, and I was forcing him out, driving him into himself, tearing down his chance to have his father proud of him.

"Then, this last summer when I came home from college with a wife and new baby, I even forced him out of his own room. We took over his room and drove him into the small den downstairs.

"You say a lot of things because you're still a family and you want to heal the wounds of others. The more you can convince them that it was your fault and not theirs, the less would be the burden on them. It was all very generous and kind and, in the end, useless. Craig was dead, and the frightening truth was, in a way, all of us had killed him."

The inevitable question emerged: What was to be done about it?

17

When the Reverend Charles R. Brace of the old Saint John's Episcopal Church in Chew's Landing heard the news of the two suicides on Thursday, he tried to place the youngsters. The names were familiar, for both the Badialis and the Foxes were members of the congregation, but he was not familiar with either child.

He would have liked to have known them all, to have every teen-ager in his parish a regular on Sunday and a devoted worker in the youth group, spreading the word that only through God can man achieve true peace. He could find only dubious comfort in the thought that their rejection of this word had led to the tragedy; and when he heard that it was linked to the Peace Moratorium, this became all the more apparent.

The Reverend Brace was originally a New Yorker, having gone through the public school system in Manhattan and graduated from New York University in 1951, then divinity school in Connecticut. His father had been an entrepreneur of sorts, though not an eminently successful one, his last major venture (with sugar cane in Barbados) ending his career. The young Brace saw the fruitlessness of such material pursuits and had turned to the ministry.

He was a tall, good-looking man in his mid-thirties with the beginnings of an expansive mid-section. His manner was remarkably forthright, his outspoken opinions freely expressed. Indeed, his whole style exuded a self-assurance that reflected his true belief in a cause—his faith in his faith in God.

He seemed little concerned with worldly things. His rectory was small and poorly furnished, and with two young children (and a third on the way) rolling around the tacky living room in a sea of toys, his home was anything but a show place. Brace himself was less than meticulous about his own appearance; it simply meant too little to him, and he would pace the littered room with total concentration, ordering his mind to be oblivious to this totally disordered ambiance. If the sight of it offended some, others found it an indication of the genuine quality of his faith. It was, perhaps, ironic that though he preached a devotion to the most patriotic image of his country, the United States flag that hung prominently outside the rectory was flagrantly torn, violating all regulations as to its display.

The reverend's religious message to his congregation was, as he put it, "the message of Christ crucified," that man was born in sin and would live in constant contest with evil, that there had always been war and rumors of war and always would be, for such was the nature of man. There could never be earthly peace, only God's peace. He was deeply influenced by the noted Episcopalian minister of Saint Stephen's Church in Philadelphia, the Reverend Alfred W. Price, whose power to heal the sick had turned him into a nationally known religious figure. ("O Lord, take my mind and think through it. Take my heart and set it on fire with love. Take these hands and through them bring to these, Thy suffering children, the fullness of Thy healing power.") Brace, himself, had studied this "laying on of hands" technique, acquired a passion for it, and recently had begun to practice its healing power over ailing congregants. For those who had unsatisfactory results from normal medical therapy, there was usually an eager response.

Brace was also a political man, his right-wing orientation as outspoken as his Fundamentalist religious beliefs. He stood four-square in favor of the government's position on the Vietnam war, and publicly stated his aversion to seeking peace through demonstration and protest. The recent Moratorium was, to him, a symbol of sickness.

There was, as he put it, "too much bad news on TV, in the newspapers. Not enough emphasis on the good. This presents a very disruptive picture of America to youth . . . gives them a morbid view of things. If the mass media sent out more good news, people would make less of the evils . . ." and, presumably, no one would protest for there would be no cause for protest, and all would be at peace.

At the same time, Brace's sermons were rich with the doctrine that man was, indeed, a sinner, that there was nothing but turmoil in the world as a result of it.

("I talked with Reverend Brace a few times," one youth said. "He said he wanted to talk to kids, but he really doesn't, he only wants to preach to us. If you challenge him on anything, sooner or later he gets around to calling you a pink.")

The news of the suicides was exceedingly distressing to him, knowing how deep would be the bereavement of the families. It was, of course, his duty to be there for them, to succor them through their anguish, and to create the proper ritual for burial. It would not be an uncomplicated problem; suicides never were in the eyes of the church. Besides, the mystery of the letters intrigued him. What, exactly, had those two sad children written? And this peace business: it suggested radicalism, yet he knew that neither set of parents would share their children's apparent antiwar persuasion.

It was, then, with considerable anxiety that he went, unsummoned, to visit the grieving parents on Thursday afternoon. To Bernie Badiali, Jr., his arrival was considerably less than consoling. Months later, he would trouble himself to write of it, laying bare his special anguish at the way the reverend came to distort the meaning of his brother's death:

My first impression of Reverend Brace came at the age of eighteen when, upon graduation from high school, I needed a letter of reference from a clergyman to get into college. Mr. Brace seemed to me then the ruler of some unseen monarchy by the way he blurted out instructions from an overstuffed chair in his living room.

"Sit down and tell me who you are," he said with little expression in his voice.

So I explained to him the nature of my visit and he gave me a pencil and a piece of unlined paper. At this, to my surprise, he began to dictate as though I were his personal stenographer:

"To Whom It May Concern:

I have served at this parish for only a short time and I know very little about Bernard. I have been assured, however, by my parishioners that he is a good Episcopalian and a fine citizen.

Sincerely yours,
Reverend C. Brace"

Almost immediately after he finished the dictation he asked what I would major in at college. It was his habit to do that, pile one sentence right into another with barely a pause. The abruptness of his dialogue kept me further on edge, especially since I wasn't sure of my major as yet. I told him history, or something. And when I told him that the school (Brevard) was of Methodist affiliation, he looked as though he would take back what I had written a moment before.

I nervously thanked him and excused myself. . . .

After our meeting, I felt obligated to attend services that Sunday if for no other reason than to show my appreciation. I recall how empty the fine old church was compared to when the former pastor, Father Bloxham, was there. Also how the service had been changed—especially the chants, for in any Episcopal service, if the chants are not satisfying, the service will suffer immeasurably. Everyone else seemed to be unenthusiastic as well. I thought that it was a sad thing, but I really didn't concern myself with it. I was going away to college and it mattered little to me.

In the next two years, I made three visits to his parish, all of which were more unrewarding that the first. The congregation had fallen off by over half and those who remained tried vainly to get themselves enthused. . . .

So it was that when, on that tortured Thursday of Craig's death, his black 1965 Rambler sedan pulled up in front of my house and he walked quickly up on the porch, gave two sharp raps on the door with one hand while he pushed it open with the other, announcing himself as he did, "Father Brace!", I felt a quickening twist in my stomach.

He stood tall in our small living room, his young-looking face out-of-kilter . . . with his barrel chest and narrow shoulders, . . . and when one saw his smooth-skinned face, his dark wavy hair, he seemed anything but a minister. A truant officer, I thought. I was aware of my bias as I looked at him, remembering how much I liked his predecessor for his warmth and friendship.

He moved into the room, first approaching my aunt and clumsily asked her if she were Mrs. Badiali. My aunt pointed to the end of our long sofa where my mother was seated. I recall that even in the anguish of that moment, my mother looked up and regarded the man with a great show of respect. It seemed odd to me, perhaps because I had never seen my mother in the presence of any minister before. He saw that look and it gave him the courage to proceed. He stood over her bent, exhausted body and said in his normally stern tone of voice: "Would you care to pray?"

. . . It was an instant that came to typify the unreality of his contact with this whole matter. For one thing, Craig, I believe, felt much the same way about religion as I did, that the Christian idea is a very beautiful thing because it contains the concepts of brotherhood and peace. There was, however, that part we couldn't accept: the punishment for "sins" and the consequent wrath of the deity. Yet on the

very day he died, there was Brace in our home to
give my family the benefit of Trinity and the remission of sins.

For another, my mother had never been a church-
goer, and for this she was laden with guilt. For years
she had talked about how bad a person she was for
not going to church, that old way of thinking: if
you go to church every Sunday, you're good, and if
you don't, you're not. It was, then, easy to understand that at Craig's death she was especially vul-
nerable in this area. So when Father Brace appeared, Mom immediately acted as if the Deity
Himself had arrived to pass judgment upon her.

"Would you care to pray?" he said to her.

It could not but distress me.

Brace remained there for over four hours, delivering
all the proper words of consolation and condolence. And
before he left, it became customary that he would lead
them all in prayer, and they bent heads as he delivered
the benediction. He went to the Foxes', where it was
much the same, though he sensed their resentment at
young Bernard's statement to the press that Joan had
died as a martyr for peace. What with their own son,
Raymond, currently serving in Vietnam, he could readily
sympathize with their aversion to any suggestion that
their daughter was allied to such an unpatriotic cause.

At the same time, he was struck by the tremendous
interest generated by the entire nation. The extent of
newspaper and television coverage that had descended on
Blackwood amazed and excited him. These had not been
particularly successful years for him. Though he had
worked hard and diligently, his congregation had
dwindled, and their enthusiasm for his message had been
less than gratifying. The beautiful old church appeared
less dignified by its tradition than worn by age while all
around this rapidly expanding community there was a
vitality that seemed to be passing him by. Now, suddenly, this tragedy. A tragedy, yes, but something more,

perhaps, something to be properly shared, to be interpreted, to be somehow turned into a constructive force. He would be less than human if he did not see the possibilities of a forum that would dignify his voice far beyond his immediate congregation.

It followed that the problem of Craig Badiali's request for cremation and avoidance of normal funeral procedure would immediately occupy his attention. Though it was not for him to decide, he was, however, ready to advise the bereaved family what he considered to be appropriate Episcopal ritual for such an occasion, and in the process, to impress upon them the desirability of presenting a devout image.

The Badialis, meanwhile, pondered the whole funeral question, taking stock of all the substantial reasons for a regular ceremony and burial, Craig's last wishes notwithstanding. They could not help but lean toward the respectability of Reverend Brace's advice rather than adding cremation to whatever stigma the suicide might have produced.

Moreover, there was another, completely unrelated reason for a normal funeral. "When Mom had her first child, it lived to be two weeks old. Mom stayed in the hospital all the time since it was known that the delivery had been faulty. The baby died of pneumonia, but she never saw the infant laid out. She never really faced that death openly. Years later even, she would mention it in some strange way, as though in wonder and speculation. It seemed proper, then, that we have a viewing of Craig's body, to have her see it, no matter what else it might do to her.

"We also decided that, because of Mom, only members of the immediate family would be invited. My father wanted it that way. But it meant that none of Craig's friends would be allowed there. . . .

"In the end, Brace had his way about the ceremony. My mom preferred it that way, she wanted to go along with the reverend. We were all so ignorant of Episcopal ritual, we really didn't have much of a choice, I suppose. When you think back on it, how could it have been otherwise at a time like that?"

Brace continued to be a frequent visitor at both the Badiali and Fox homes. Bernie would write of it:

"Father Brace!" came the throaty voice from the front door, and he'd walk into the kitchen where we'd usually be sitting. Our door was never locked, so we'd never know when he might walk in. On this occasion, he presented himself in our midst before we had a chance to rise in greeting.

"I've been up all night and I think God and I have reached a conclusion as to what to tell the press."

He had, as I remembered, been up all the previous night too and had come to an earlier conclusion that "we must not release any statements to the press until I've ordered my mind completely!" which, of course, had been aimed at my comments that Craig had done this out of his desire for peace.

"Instead of a protest for peace," he went on, "we'll call it a protest for God's peace, and instead of a Moratorium on war, we'll call it a Moratorium on sin." He sat there with his arms folded across his chest looking as though he would burst with excitement. "Yes, I've been up all night preparing the statement for the press. I've even talked it over with the bishop and I have his go-ahead."

It was a point at which my rising anger was suddenly dampened by disbelief. The man is unreal, I thought. It was just two days since the suicides and he was telling us that he had reached a miraculous decision that would resolve everything. I was thinking that he didn't even know Craig, he didn't know what this was all about.

I felt my wife's hand resting gently on my shoulder. My mother was pouring him a cup of tea and I could see how happy she was for his presence.

There was, then, nothing I could say.

18

As on every school day, on Friday, October 17, 1969, the bell rang at eight and the voice of the principal, Mrs. Virginia Forneron, resounded over the loudspeaker piped into every room in the building. The students rose in their home rooms in response, turned toward the American flag that stood in the appropriate corner and, in unison, together with their unseen principal, delivered the Pledge of Allegiance.

There were also announcements, generally concentrating on breaches of discipline. The administration used this time to advise the students on any matters it deemed necessary.

On the matter of Craig Badiali and Joan Fox, not one word was mentioned.

Commented Steve Karras: "It was like something out of a spook movie. Not one teacher brought it up. You could go from one class period to the next, and it was like this thing had never happened. And then it began to sink in: this was official school policy."

There was, of course, talk in the halls and in home rooms between periods, quiet talk among the students. Then there were teachers like Mrs. Wagner and Mr. Di Ponziano whose anguish was very much in evidence, whose voices were choked by periodic spasms of emotion. There were other teachers, Mr. Fischer in the basement shop for manual arts, for one, who was less than patient with Liz Quemore: "You're crying over nothing . . . I didn't think you were that sort. . . ." Mostly, however, it was a day of silence, the sounds in the halls were subdued, the students generating this show of respect, one day wherein they would acknowledge the tragedy without leadership from anyone. The silence of the administration was not kin to the silence of the students.

"This school is a sick joke," said Desi Worland in a rage. "If there was ever any doubt about it, it was gone on Friday."

To Stanley Pietrowksi, the cynic, it was a day to spread the word about the candlelight march for the coming Wednesday, though he anticipated no great turnout. Yet there were many who agreed to come, as long as it was not violating any rules, they said. Stanley was impressed: "Kids who had never joined a demonstration in their lives said they would come. I had to admit, it really started to grow."

The march committee was, indeed, functioning well. Several members met with the mayor himself, who agreed that such a memorial service was not out of order as long as there would be absolutely no publicity of any kind, and that the press would be denied any advance notice of it. This was the essence of the problem, the mayor stipulated: publicity was apt to bring the undesirable element, radicals, bearded hippies, and so forth, who would come from the outside to disrupt, perhaps even be dangerously violent. "We don't want any of those peace demonstrations in Blackwood," he said.

A friend of Craig's, John Millet, Jr., went to see the Reverend John Costas of the Presbyterian Church on the corner of Church Street and the Black Horse Pike, hoping that he would serve as chaplain for the event. Costas was a compassionate man with a special feeling for young people. Originally from New York, his background was not without a certain distinction for his profession, albeit a disturbing one: formerly an alcoholic, he had spent sixteen months in a mental institution, a somewhat demeaning experience he had not been ashamed to expose, for he had found his calling out of the anguish of it. It was his aim to help people in trouble, and his time was always open to the needs of others. "I have conducted over six hundred private counselings in the three years I have spent in Blackwood."

Mr. Costas liked to think of himself as a modern man. Not long before this tragedy, he had run a religious parade in town under the banner of his own version of those notorious initials, LSD—Love. Salvation. Dedication. With a singular flair, he had dressed himself in the costume of a hippie; beads, a flamboyantly colored shirt, a vast shock of false hair. Salvation Sam, he called himself, and he preached to his congregation to get high on spirit for a renewal of faith in Christianity. "There is so much to be gained by a devotion to God, it is being wasted by the way we ignore it. We are simply not using what we already have."

The Reverend Costas was sympathetic to young Millet's request and consented to be part of this ceremony. He was, however, as sensitive to its complications as was the mayor, noting the danger of an invading swarm of dissident kids from as far away as Camden, even Philadelphia. Nor was he certain he wanted to lend his name to the commemoration of an event that was so positively linked to the Vietnam protest, for he himself was not in opposition to his government's program.

Besides, he noted, neither Craig nor Joan was a member of his congregation. In fact, he did not know either of them or their families.

Nevertheless—though he was not certain what it all meant nor how he might speak of it from his pulpit—he agreed to join the march. What he did not know at the time was that he was the only one of the several ministers asked who was willing to do so.

On Friday evening, the gathering of teen-age mourners shifted from the Quemores' to the home of Stanley Pietrowski, whose parents were accustomed to going away on weekends. A small group gathered there, including Chan and Liz Quemore, Desi Worland, Charlie Kean, John Millet, Bill Billhardt. To Liz, it was an evening more painful than she was prepared for. "We sat around and played records. Nobody said very much, but everyone was thinking about them. We'd heard about those twenty-four letters and I guess everybody must have thought about that, wondering who they had written to. I didn't think Craig had written me, but I wouldn't have been surprised if he had. I just couldn't think why they didn't give those letters out, that's all, and I guess that upset me too. I sat there and let the music get to me.

Stanley had a Joni Mitchell record Craig liked; Craig would play it over and over. There was one song he liked more than the others: 'Marcy.' He liked it so much, when we went out together, he would call me Marcy. I had spent an hour preparing myself for the sound of that song, and then, when it came, I bit my lip trying to hold it all back. But I couldn't. I just started to crack up and it was awful. I couldn't stay any longer. I didn't think how far it was to my own house; I guess it was miles away and it was dark. I cried and walked, and then John Millet came for me in his car and took me home. It was a long time before I could listen to that song again."

It was that kind of night, tender and sweet and painful in memory. There was Bill Billhardt, class leader, dramatics co-worker and loyal friend to Craig, who, like Liz, could not bear the extent of his anguish and had to run from the scene. They were different kinds of kids with completely different points of view. John Millet, for example, had a strong yearning to become a soldier to fight in Vietnam. "I lost a good friend in that war!" he had said, and there was Desi, the plaintive, suffering, indomitable Desi, who quietly replied: "So did I," and cried for Craig, while sympathizing with John whose grief was akin to hers.

Elsewhere in Blackwood, in the merchants' world beyond the kids, in the stores and supermarkets, in the taverns and service stations, there was no comparable show of emotion. Those who knew the parents would speak of their suffering and others would shake their hands in sympathy. *Courier-Post* reporter Thom Akeman went cruising through the area and tried to gauge the prevailing mood: "There was a jerk of the head, a fixed eye, a silent voice every time the word 'suicide' was mentioned," he wrote. "But mostly, people explained, they cannot accept Joan Fox and Craig Badiali as martyrs. They can't believe the seventeen-year-olds died Wednesday for what they said—peace and brotherhood. There has to be another explanation for the suicides, they say. An easier, more forgettable reason . . . something trite and comprehensible. Something authorities say doesn't exist.

". . . A cashier in a grocery store, a woman who almost daily sold chewing gum to Joan, tried to explain: '. . . It just doesn't make sense. She wasn't that type of child.'

"In a hobby shop, two boys were listening to a balding salesman reminisce about his experiences in the Second World War. The boys said they could understand how a couple could want to sacrifice their own lives to try to awaken people to the human problems around them. They said they would let Joan and Craig become martyrs. The balding salesman said No. 'They just snapped. They didn't have the courage to live.' "

The Reverend Brace continued to be troubled by the pending drama of the weekend. The presence of reporters and television people hovered over him, exacerbating his tenseness with their demands upon him. The young NBC producer, Rafael Abramovitz fascinated him. Brace, the dedicated man-on-fire with the passions of his faith in God and the majesty of America, could not resist the urge to lecture the young Jew. Not blatantly, of course. He was far too sophisticated for that. Besides, he could not help but admire Abramovitz, admire his quickness, his intelligence, his ability to function so well without sacrificing an iota of his personal identity. To Brace, it was a treat to meet a young man with the power of NBC behind him, and he wanted to make his own impact.

"He did not deny his ambitiousness," said Abramovitz. "He saw the temptation offered by national television exposure but he didn't want to do anything that others would construe to be 'calling attention to himself.' Yet he did want to be a legitimate part of the story; he wanted to speak his mind. I could see that he would be marvelous on the documentary and assured him that he would have the right to say whatever he wanted. You could see all the wheels turning as he walked around the room, fussing with one thing or another. He was thinking about his sermon and wanted to tell me about it. I got the feeling that he even wanted my advice."

Brace *was* troubled about the sermon. What stand

should he take? How much of a judgment must be made on the suicides? What should be his message? If he could not praise the two children for their tragic act, it was absolutely essential that he extend "comfort and consolation to the parents," as the bishop had advised. On one hand, he was much too committed as a preacher to wash it all away with meaningless piety he knew others might resort to. On the other, it was essential that he "walk the tightrope" between condemning and condoning the act.

"Left-wingers are everywhere," he told Abramovitz. "Moratoriums are really left-wing plots to upset teenagers. They get all these kids worked up merely to take them away from the church. This SDS business—I'm not at all convinced they aren't active at Highland High School. I'm not at all convinced that the SDS weren't really responsible for this thing."

"He did not think there was a dope problem with the kids. No pregnancy, either," Abramovitz noted. "He felt the suicides were the result of a devilish conspiracy against God and America."

It was the kind of meat that made a tasty television stew.

The leading funeral home in the area was run by Edward C. Gardner on the Black Horse Pike in nearby Runnemede, and the Badialis turned to him to handle the affair. (The Foxes, meanwhile, lived closer to Charles McCann's funeral home on Church Street. They would be forced to delay the ceremony until the return of Joan's brother Raymond, on duty in the army. The two funerals would be separate.)

When mortician Edward Gardner picked up the body of Craig Badiali at the medical examiner's office, he was immediately aware that he would have problems with the embalming process: frequently, with death caused by carbon monoxide poisoning, the body tissue begins to decompose with infectious bacteria, eating away tissues that can seriously disfigure a corpse. It was a delicate matter, for a proper embalming must recreate the face of the deceased with sufficient accuracy. Anything less becomes distasteful and reflects badly on the mortician.

Since he had not known Craig alive, he had no choice

but to call Bernard, the brother—for he had to know how much deterioration had occurred around the nose and mouth.

Bernie was stunned by the call. He had reached a plateau of contained anguish, unable to conceive of anything worse that he might have to experience until the funeral itself on Monday. Now this call, this frightening summons to present himself where he least wanted to go, to see what he least wanted to see, to add torture to his torment in behalf of a demonstration he himself did not even endorse. Yet he knew he would have to go—if for no other purpose than to please his mother and her need to have this final look at Craig. He went, thinking how painfully grotesque was this duty, aware of a strange sense of foreboding that the funeral was wrong from the start, that something dreadful was going to happen as a result of it.

"I tried to protect myself, saying it really wasn't such a terrible thing. Mr. Gardner seemed like a very decent man. I guess I thought funeral directors were a bunch of stiff-shirted phonies in dark blue suits who spent their lives trying to put on a properly glum look. But I liked Mr. Gardner. He needed my help, I told myself, so I went."

Not surprisingly, reporter Thom Akeman of the *Courier-Post* heard of the memorial candlelight march scheduled for the coming Wednesday. Unaware of any requests for secrecy, he featured this coming event in his piece for Saturday, quoting an unidentified boy as his source: "They believed in something very strongly. I'm sure they thought their deaths were going to be effective . . . Wednesday night will see whether or not they are martyrs."

It was all Blackwoodians needed. It was as if they were waiting for some such exposure as an excuse to attack. The article proved perfect for this, replete with such loaded words as "candlelight march . . . memorial . . . peace . . . martyrdom." Visions of ten thousand radical-hippie-protesting-long-haired out-of-towners chanting the phrases of revolution, raising angry fists in the face of network television cameras!

Dozens of phones began ringing—all over Gloucester Township.

There were two special visitors to Blackwood that weekend: Drs. Berkley Hathorne and Paul Curtis of the Suicide Prevention Unit, a department of the National Institute of Mental Health at Bethesda, Maryland. It was their policy to speak to bereaved families immediately after such tragedies when emotions were still on the surface, probing for as much understanding of the case as was possible, at the same time offering whatever advice and succor that were within their power. Their primary mission, however, was to learn as much of the cause as was possible, to avoid any immediate danger of an epidemic.

There is enough in the literature of suicides to support such fears. Well-publicized deaths such as Craig and Joan's sometimes influenced others who are pausing on the brink. When Marilyn Monroe died of an overdose of barbiturates, there was an alarming increase of similar feminine suicide attempts in various parts of the Western world. In the matter of teen-agers, the fear was even more urgent. (In the eighteenth century, Goethe's *The Sorrows of Young Werther,* a novel that became extremely popular throughout the world, was believed to have initiated a wave of schoolboy suicides in Germany shortly after its publication. Goethe himself suffered many denunciations, and the book was banned in some cities. There are still critical references to "Wertherism.")

Although suicides among American adolescents has never been a problem of staggering dimensions, it is seldom without a tragic impact far in excess of comparable acts by adults. Besides, it is an ever-increasing problem in our times. (From 1952 to 1962, e.g., the incidence of teen-age suicides rose 35 per cent among whites and 82 per cent among nonwhites.)

Suicides are listed as the fourth leading cause of teen-age death, behind accidents (53 per cent), cancer (12 per cent) and homicide (4.3 per cent). If the suicide figure appears insignificant (barely 500 cases reported annually), one can only estimate how many deaths listed as accidents are actually suicidally induced or are interpreted as accidents to protect the family name. There are three times as many boy victims as girls, though ten times as many girls make the attempt. Boys tend to resort to firearms and hanging; most girls use poison. It is believed that almost all adolescents who are potential suicides send out signals of their despair: extreme depressions, loss of appetite, excessive drinking, wild driving, antisociability, sleeplessness. A cry for help, as it were.

It is also statistically evident that most teen-age suicides have older brothers and sisters, and not the opposite.

However, there was almost nothing in Craig and Joan's history to indicate that suicide was imminent. They had, in effect, sent out no special "cry for help." Most teen-age suicides derive from such general causes as quarrels with parents, broken romances, failure in school, illegitimate pregnancies, poor health, troubles with the law. With Craig and Joan, no such problems were involved. Dr. Louis Dublin, a leading contributor to the growing literature of suicides, once observed: "Some psychiatrists have declared that all suicide victims are psychotic and that no 'normal' persons actually destroy themselves. This view seems hard to reconcile with such cases in which suicide appears to have been the outcome of considerable reasoning." Wrote Dr. Klaus Berblinger of the University of California School of Medicine: "Self-destruction is not (always) regarded as the result of a disordered mind." And the philosopher William James: "I take it that no man who is educated has not dallied with the thought of suicide."

The late Karen Horney, psychiatrist and author, believed that the heart of all neurotic development was what she chose to call "the search for glory," a theme expanded upon by Dr. Louis De Rosis: "Suicide represents the outcome of a severe frustration of a person's search for glory. (Correspondingly, the world is in its present throes of self-destruction for precisely the same reason. Each nation is locked in a pursuit of glory unmindful of their basic humaneness, the basic tenderness that all of us require for growth and well being.) . . . Despite conflicting and suppressive attitudes toward a child who is not altogether crushed, the desire for that child to enlarge himself will continue to be arrested. In his mind, he becomes a hero, a great achiever. If, however, he attempts to make real these inner heroics, he runs the risk of facing his failure—and this can lead to suicide. When a person fails in this pursuit of glory as dictated by his fantasy ["Maybe this will start a chain reaction of peace, love, and communication . . ."], he is confronted with another feeling, the design of which is to *compel* allegiance to this pursuit. . . ."

There were no psychiatrists residing in Blackwood, no traditions of therapeutic consultations. People in trouble were left with ministers or sympathetic "Dutch Uncles." To bright, exceptionally sensitive kids like Craig and Joan, this was insufficient. As their friend Ann Schramm pointed out with extraordinary perceptivity: "Craig needed someone outstanding to talk to, someone inspirational who could put things in proper perspective. He had so much compassion of his own to give, it was hard for him to get it back. His demands on life were great. He felt that people didn't care enough for each other, they didn't respond to each other. He was unsure about his own potential and he didn't know how to adjust to his confusions and frustrations. He really needed professional help.

"I would guess that he needed Joan to go through with it. She was so devoted to him, she could not have let him die without her. Without Craig, she had no one to whom she could really give herself, even be herself. She was so confused. She just didn't want to go on living without him.

"One could almost picture the way it might have happened: Craig gets terribly depressed over the way things are going and can't find surcease anywhere, and then he tells Joan he thinks he really wants to die. She cries and tells him 'if you do, I want to, too! . . .' "

Dr. Sabert Basescu, psychologist at New York University Graduate School of Arts and Sciences, after reviewing the available material on Craig and Joan, made this comment: "Certainly Craig's impotence in confronting his family, his future, and the world provided a fertile ground for his suicide, but his notes sug-

gested a deeper meaning to the act—an intensive need
to counteract that impotence itself. Craig's suicide might
be viewed as an expression of his impotence on one hand,
and the heroic hope that his death could be the instru-
mentality for dramatic change on the other. His death
cannot be explained as simply an expression of personal
pathology. In such times of world crisis and a nation's
insanity, there are, hopefully, cries of protest."

Much of this became known to the two specialists from
Bethesda as they probed among the intimates of the two
kids. They were the only strangers who spoke with the
bereaved parents. In addition, they interviewed relatives,
neighbors, friends, officials, ministers, all of which was
kept confidential.

Their recommendations were significant: It would be
unwise to release the suicide notes lest their recipients
overreact to the poignant message. It would be equally
unwise to encourage martyrdom for the two. It would be
far better if the tragedy were forgotten as quickly as
possible.

It was, the two specialists made clear, merely a rec-
ommendation, a precautionary tactic to avoid any recur-
rence. However, it so perfectly reflected the desires of
the families, the local officials, the school administration,
and the bewildered citizenry that it could not have
been more effectively implemented if it had been a local
law itself.

It can be assumed that this betrayal of Craig and
Joan's intent did not escape the two specialists, or that
the impounding of the twenty-four suicide notes was a
terribly frustrating action to the many dozens more, each
of whom might have anticipated that one had been written to him. Indeed, this policy of denying their martyrdom, of curtailing the flowering of whatever meaning
might be attributed to their deaths, turned out to be as
much a source of frustration as pacification.

The letters . . . the letters. "If the two kids wanted
them to be read, they should have mailed them," commented the medical examiner, Thomas Daley. It was a
question that brought on a spate of speculations. For
those who knew Craig and Joan (and apparently hundreds of others from all over the country), the thought

that their suicide notes would not be delivered would never have entered their minds. There was a terrible contradiction implicit in this betrayal, for they were giving up their lives to dramatize the failure of others to love and communicate. That it struck home to many was indicated by the quantity of mail in protest. It was seen as another example of how horrible life must have been for them. For Craig and Joan to make an impact (the whole purpose of their deaths), were they supposed to mail their suicide notes a day in advance to be certain they arrived in time for the discovery? Indeed, psychiatrists are the first to admit that almost all suicide attempts—no matter how determined—are at least partly predicated on the possibility of failure, to say nothing of the omnipresent chance that they might change their minds at the last minute.

Daley's mail included the following:

I have just read with disbelief an account in the *New York Times* of your response to the final wishes of the two young people who died so that their country might live. The twenty-four notes they left were intended to be read by the twenty-four people. . . . If you refuse to release these notes to such people their deaths are made a joke.

I cannot imagine a more preposterous ending to these two young lives than the deliberate withholding of these letters. What right—legal, moral, or human—do you have to deny their message exposure?

I understand that you are withholding the letters of the twin suicides. I believe that is a sensitive even benevolent thing to do. I know that if a friend of mine committed suicide, I would not have the slightest curiosity as to what he wrote me in his final hour. More power to you, Mr. Daley. If you play your cards right, maybe you can make some real money out of selling them to a magazine. P.S.: Please withhold this letter from my parents.

Daley was unjustly criticized. "I did not withhold these letters. In fact, I was reprimanded for letting the press get their hands on a few of them. I did what any official would do: I simply turned them over to the proper authorities."

He had no idea of what happened to them after he left them with the county medical examiner, Dr. Louis Reigert, at the Pennsauken Morgue. He did not have the authority to do otherwise. Besides, he was in a considerable hurry to wind up his affiliation with the tragedy, having long since arranged with friends to go to northern Maine for a weekend hunting trip.

"Hunting is my big hobby," said Daley. "That and golf. I collect guns and like to use them. In fact, I was so eager to get moving on this trip, I became impatient with those two psychiatrists. I mean, it was just another round of the same questions over and over. I really had nothing to add to what everybody knew or did not know. It was a sad business, all right. I felt sorry for the parents and all, but this was getting out of hand. Everybody was making such a big thing out of it. I face suicides all the time, hundreds of them a year. Only a month or so before, a young girl rolled off the top of a tall apartment building in Cherry Hill, left a note and all, but there was none of this fuss afterward.

"I can tell you, it was a pleasure getting out of town that Saturday morning. We drove all the way up to Maine. It was like a wilderness up there, so when I got this message that my wife had called, I was very worried; it scared hell out of me. It turned out that my answering service had a message that there was a telegram for me —from a bunch of students in North Carolina who didn't like what had happened with those letters."

The problem of the letters would grow in the wake of the tragedy. Since those who grieved the most were the most likely recipients, they were at first too overcome to be concerned about it. However, it would work its way slowly into their consciousness as the shock of the deaths began to subside. Who had them? To whom were they written? And the rumors that worked their way into public knowledge only served to excite ever-increasing speculations.

Stanley Pietrowski said: "I've got problems about this, but I'm not even sure of the questions. They won't give out those notes and it's really hard to understand why. You think, What was in them that makes them so dangerous? I think one thing: I'll bet that Craig wrote one of those notes to the President of the United States. He would do a thing like that. Write the President and tell him why he was killing himself. . . ."

Debbie Gliick had equally confused reactions. She felt that Joan must have written to her, but it frightened her that maybe she didn't, maybe Joan chose not to, and Debbie did not want to face that. Then too, perhaps Joan had written things to her that she would not want to read, that the letter would not satisfy her at all. She began to have fantasies about all these alternatives: Joan meant so much to her, she could not work her way out of it. She would think about those letters for months.

It was never out of mind. Desi Worland would curse the authorities for this denial. When the rumor spread some weeks after that the letters had been destroyed, she could only comment: "What did they think was in them: secrets of the H-Bomb?"

On Sunday morning, the Reverend Brace crossed the old Black Horse Pike from the rectory to the historic Saint John's Episcopal Church, having prepared himself for the challenge of the Lord's day. It would begin at seven-thirty a.m. with the early worship service, through the nine-fifteen a.m. family worship, and culminate with the principal service at eleven-fifteen, wherein the sermon would be delivered. If he expected a large turn-out as a result of the weekend dramatics, he must have been a disappointed man: at the high point of the morning, there were barely twenty people present, including his wife (who was organist) and the choir. It was as if the congregation sensed the pending challenge of the sermon and chose to avoid it, preferring to have the whole tragic affair buried with the two children. The reverend, however, had the sturdy capacity to speak to twenty with no less fervor than he would to an audience of twenty million on national television, for his tone was never without passion, one would guess, even when sipping tea with his wife.

Bernie Badiali, Jr., was there on that morning, though he was not at all sure what drove him to attend. "I knew I wouldn't find peace, even with the organ and sunlight through the stained glass windows of that marvelous old church. It would be anything but peaceful for me. I guess I just wanted to hear what Reverend Brace would say. It would be about Craig and I simply had to know.

"He began talking about the peace symbol, the V symbol, the two fingers held erect, saying it was a pagan symbol, a defiant rebellious worldly symbol. He wanted it changed to the sign of the cross, and he held up two fingers, one from each hand, and crossed them. He said that this is what young people should be showing to the world. He got himself all strung out on the point, for almost half an hour, it seemed, over and over, bad-mouthing kids who held up the V."

It was God's peace that the reverend was calling for. The message of Christ crucified again, that there will always be war for that is the nature of man. "There will never be peace between man and man until there is a godly peace between all men and God." The answer to the problems of young people lay primarily in their failure to achieve such a peace. "Do you really want true and godly peace? Well, pray for God's peace again and again and again."

To Bernie, once again, "it was unbelievable" that Brace should thus use his brother's death to preach a sermon that violated the avowed purpose of that death. In all the Christian era, was there ever a war when the cross was not carried as a standard by both warring factions? The ironies were piling up on Bernie. Ironies and contradictions, one on top of another. It could be said that in the past year or two, Craig had become an agnostic, perhaps even because of this man; now this same man was, in his way, condemning Craig for the very virtues he had given his life for. Bernie felt that pieces of his brother's death were being chipped off and discarded, the meaning of it distorted, his message to the world twisted. "Was this what it all came down to, this contest over how to hold up your fingers?" Craig, the

beautiful dove-like agnostic, was being used by this pious
symbol of the hawk. Craig, the hater of funerals and
viewings and ceremony, was to be buried in the warp of
the very patterns he despised. What hurt Bernie even
more was his own acquiescence, that somehow, he had
let too much of this happen, the pressures of the living
had conspired to overwhelm him.

It was about this hour, over seven hundred miles away
on an island near Portage, Maine, that the hunter,
Thomas Daley, confronted a bear, "black and rugged,
about four hundred-fifty pounds" and he moved in on it,
cocked his .44 Magnum pistol until he stood no more
than forty yards away, then felled the animal with one
shot.

"I'd never shot a bear before . . ." he said.

In the suburb of Collingswood, just outside of Camden, a few minutes' drive from Blackwood, the well-
known aging minister, Dr. Carl McIntyre, head of the
Fundamentalist International Council of Christian
Churches, issued a ringing statement condemning the
suicides of Joan Fox and Craig Badiali. ". . . The glori-
fication of their evil deed by making them martyrs could
stimulate emulation. The Moratorium with its call for
immediate and unconditional withdrawal from Vietnam
constitutes surrender to the communists. Our boys who
have died in battle for their country, flag, and freedom
deserve all honor. To use their names and death as the
Moratorium marches do against the cause they gave the
full measure of their devotion for is a sacrilege. To
lead youth to feel that such a sacrifice is vain and wrong
makes them a comfort to our enemy and the disciples of
a false peace. . . . The Second Bible Believers March on
Trenton next Saturday will challenge youth to the cause
of victory we must have and will seek to clear up their
confusion and despair. . . ."

The candlelight memorial march for Craig and Joan,
meanwhile, was canceled by a number of the youths who
had helped to organize it, worried that the press report
"would attract outsiders who might turn the plain,

simple service into a peace demonstration. . . . It would be hypocritical."

Said the ever-volatile Desi Worland: "We can't have a march. They won't give us the letters the two had written. The school insists on silence. We can't go to Craig's funeral. They think it makes us forget, but it only makes us mad."

The news of the cancellation of the march was very upsetting to at least one parent. Mrs. Betty Quemore saw the despair of her children and, typically, began calling as many parents as she knew, trying to get their cooperation in organizing an action to satisfy this need for a memorial "so that the children would not feel so terribly rejected." She received only negative responses. Rebuff after rebuff. "By late Sunday night, I'd had it. There was hardly an adult in Blackwood who would have anything to do with it. . . ."

The Quemore kids decided to have their own service on Wednesday. They would let it be known at school that this was going to happen and anyone who wished to come was welcome. They would make no special invitations, no announcements, no phone calls, even.

It would be something. At least there would be something.

19

Monday, October 20, the day of the Badiali funeral, began sunny and warm and sweet-smelling, an Indian-summer day. The family rose early, as was their custom, but the silence among them was rooted in a terrible anxiety that had been growing throughout the weekend. Though they did not speak of it, each was worried about how the others would respond and all of them were doubly concerned about the mother.

It had been decided that the viewing of Craig's body would span as brief a time as possible. A half-hour, starting at nine o'clock, to be immediately followed by the funeral ceremony. It was to be a small intimate affair, only close family and a few friends were invited. No teen-agers, as noted, not even Craig's closest friends, who were, in fact, specifically advised not to come. All this was out of deference to Dolly Badiali. She was to see the body of her son with the understanding that she would not stay for the funeral or attend the final interment.

Bernie was especially nervous about her, having seen her literally break apart on that first day of agony, knowing he could never forget his own horror at the extent of it. Indeed, she was always in his mind and he struggled to contain his own grief lest any release of it might trigger another wave of hers. "I would sometimes feel that choking emotion that precedes a flood of tears, and I would go off alone somewhere, in a room, in my car for a ride, a walk, maybe. For one thing, your pride bids you do that—I didn't even want my wife to see me —and then you let it out, the wailing, the crying, all those insane gestures one does when the agony becomes unbearable. Alone, yes, and certainly never in front of my mother."

Dolly Badiali was not, in any way, a sick or disturbed woman. She was much loved by her own family, and all her brothers and sisters, the large Ivins breed, all of whom lived within a few miles of each other. She was sweet-natured and even-tempered, a warm, gentle woman who made others feel comfortable, all of Craig's friends very much included. There was, in fact, a fine stable balance about her, and though she was not the sturdy earth-mother type, she seemed to have no need for any of the crutches many American women lean on as they drift into idle middle years: she was not addicted to daytime soap operas, excessive drinking, mystical interpolations or astrology, nor was she even particularly religious. She loved her family. That was sufficient. Whatever emotional problems she had to face seemed eminently copable.

Until Craig's death. Husband and son would talk about that. They could easily understand her grief, their own being compelling enough; but Dolly just didn't seem able to handle it. "It was as if something had snapped inside her," Bernie thought. "I couldn't explain it or analyze it, though I sensed it well enough. Maybe it was just my own overreaction, maybe she was no worse off than Dad or myself, but I didn't think so."

So they spent the days close by her, constantly surrounding her with the company of her family, long, random time-consuming prattle over a pot of coffee at the large kitchen table, sometimes silly talk; talk about this one or that one, the kids, the relatives; retelling old yarns such as the time when a friend was singing at a Saturday night tavern and he let a wasp fly in his mouth and sting him on the palate, how he had seen it coming right in the middle of holding a high note but never believed it would actually fly inside. They would make her smile and sometimes she would contribute a story of her own, but they all knew that she was never free of pain, that they were all playing the game together, this loving ploy for her benefit, and God knows what it was going to be like for her when she walked into that funeral home. "Even Reverend Brace became a supporting factor," Bernie said. "She seemed to look forward to his visits and found a certain relief in prayer."

So it was that the Badialis drove to Gardner's Funeral Home shortly before nine that morning, preparing themselves for their first public show of grief. To Bernie, "the tension was almost unbearable. We drove to the funeral parlor and I thought again what a heartbreaking thing this was to do to Craig, this insane viewing of his body and the ceremony after, to have violated him this way and then, on top of it, to have kept all his friends from it . . . and, for the first time, I thought that my mother must have known that all this was being done for her, that she was the cause of this part of it, and my God, how she must be suffering with that!"

As they approached Gardner's on the Black Horse Pike, they were jolted again by the sight of television cameras and crews, of newspaper reporters, and dozens of policemen and bystanders, all these abrasive forces so foreign to their lives now omnipresent at the moment of their greatest agony, intrusive at the moment of their greatest need for privacy. The Badialis wanted to usher the mother inside, just long enough to show her this final sight of her son, then usher her out—that they all might share this mutual anguish with whatever strength they could muster—but the fashioning of a public spectacle, this frightening invasion of alien eyes doomed them to some inexorable collapse. They all sensed it, and said nothing.

Edward Gardner had the police working hard and well, keeping everyone across the street from the parlor, under the façade of the Pantry Pride Supermarket. But, as Bernie was quick to note, "he couldn't keep them from filming the scene. Those TV cameras, like Peeping Toms with those zoom lenses, right into the car windows as we went by, in the parking lot, the walk to the door. They could even shoot through the parlor window. Mother and Dad sat in the car while my uncles and I talked about it out front, and we wondered, what right they had to do this? One of my uncles suggested that we go over there and tell them to go, all of them, but my dad came over and said no, it would create a bad scene and I agreed with him, I don't know why, it just felt that way, it would almost be like committing an act of violence with them, they thought they had the right to film anything they wished."

The funeral parlor was cleared for the mother's entrance and, finally, they brought her inside. "When she finally came into the room, in the presence of the casket, I could feel her body go limp. She was conscious, but she could barely stand. I was holding her on one side, my dad on the other, my uncle nearby. We brought her close to the casket and she crumbled like someone without a bone in her body. I could barely move, wondering if she were actually conscious. But she spoke, she wanted to stay there, to move even closer, she wanted us to hold her there for another moment, and then I couldn't stand it any more. I couldn't. I couldn't, no matter how hard I tried. I hated what was happening to me. I didn't want to break down in front of anyone else. My uncle saw, and he took my place, and I walked away to the wall crying again, and I just didn't know what I was going to do.

"Then I heard my mother say that she'd had enough. She was ready to leave. I guess that saved me, because I turned back to her. She was wonderfully composed, all things considered. We took her out and into the car, and I was all right again.

"All the while, the TV cameras were filming it. I hated that, hated the thought of it, but what could anyone do? The camera following us, you could see them, you could even hear them from across the street, the director telling the cameraman to do this or that. It was gruesome."

Bernie drove his mother to her sister's house in nearby Chew's Landing, under the very shadow of Saint John's Church, and took her inside, another part of the day's plan. She would spend the rest of the morning there, away from all further ceremony and confrontation. Bernie kissed her cheek and embraced her for a long moment, a silent comment to compliment her courage. There was no doubt that she had survived the scene, the worst possible scene, and that everything that followed would be easier for her.

It would not be so for Bernie.

He drove back toward the funeral parlor, and on his left as he was approaching Gardner's, he saw them again,

those same television men; and when they saw his car,
they pointed and whirled a camera to shoot its return.
It seemed like a cannon to him, zeroing in on what was
left of his equanimity. "It just didn't seem right that they
should still be around. Hadn't they gotten enough?
Hadn't they? The press and all these phone calls, the
questions, hour by hour those first few days, and now the
television, more and more of them. They'd been over at
my home taking pictures, outside the door, outside the
windows, you couldn't leave the house without confronting them. They'd been out to Bee's Lane taking shots of
the car, they'd seen it all, maybe even my breakdown
inside the chapel at Gardner's, yes, that most of all. I
didn't want anyone to see that, especially them. I'd
thought so much about that, how hard I'd determined not
to. That hurt me terribly, and they had seen it.

"I guess it was all too much for me. I cracked. . . ."

He was alone in the car. It would never have happened
otherwise, for there was nothing in his history to suggest
an aberrant act. He had never hit anyone, never tasted
a need for violence. Even in his best football years in
high school, though he was a hard-running quarterback,
his power was in his drive, never in his viciousness. But
at that instant, he swerved his car to the left against
the oncoming traffic and drove it hard across the Black
Horse Pike, up over the curb on the far side, straight at
the television camera that was backed up against the
supermarket.

The cameraman, the reporters, the bystanders were at
first too incredulous to move. A moment later, a few of
them saw the danger and scattered, letting out a sudden
whelp of anticipated tragedy.

"It was a terribly unreasoning instant, but I wasn't
going to hit them, I knew that. I just wanted to frighten
them, to let them know how I felt."

Bernie jumped out of his car to justify his rage. It was
not to be they who were the injured party: it was he,
and he demanded that status. "Get out of here!" he
hollered. "Haven't you had enough? Get out of here!"

They stood like dumb-struck statues, unable to react.
(If something had been said in return, one got the feeling
that the words might have been movie-like: "Sorry about

that, son, but we're only trying to do our job . . . .") They
didn't leave. They merely moved to a slightly more distant location—conveniently behind two heavy telephone
poles—presumably for protection in the event of Bernie's
return.

"I didn't make any apologies. I knew I should have,
but I didn't. I just drove off, back across the street to
the funeral home."

The cameras began filming again from the new van-
tage point, barely distinguishable from the other, and one
intrepid reporter hustled to a phone and reported the
entire incident. Long before Craig's body was finally
interred, the radios of Blackwood would broadcast this
distressing incident—from the point of view of those who
faced the car, not the camera.

Bernie, meanwhile, still had the funeral to cope with.

There were problems inside the parlor: the service
was supposed to start immediately, but Mr. and Mrs.
Andrew Fox had not yet arrived. Bernie waited in the
private room with his relatives, trying to contend with
the intermittent sobbing and choked voices as well as
this newly tainted image of himself. He went out to call
the Foxes, inquiring as to their tardiness, only to learn
that they had misunderstood the starting hour to be
eleven o'clock, not ten. They would come as quickly as
they could.

"I went into the gallery where the casket was, wondering how I was going to wait for this thing to finally
happen. All I could think of was the dozens of people
milling around, exactly what Craig had asked not to
have . . . again and again, it was like a recurring night-
mare."

It was close to eleven when the Fox family arrived in
a police car. The Badiali family filed into the gallery
and took seats for the service.

It was a very trying experience for Reverend Charles
Brace. Apart from the anguish he had to face, there
was the harassing problem of choosing a position from
which he could deliver his eulogy—"to walk a tightrope,"
as he had put it. At the same time, he could not deny
his fascination with the tremendous impact of the event,

knowing that the entire country was aware of it now. They would learn of what he had to say, culminating at the burial where the final eulogy would actually be filmed, while here, in this private ceremony, there were doubtless those who would take note of his message.

He stood beside the casket, holding the handwritten pages, and when he began to speak, his voice sounded more emotional than was customary. He cracked on words in the middle of sentences, sometimes stopping to reread for clarity, and for all his years of experience, tears welled up to blur his vision.

To Bernie, the horror of the day continued as the reverend droned on. "He kept turning those trembling pages, it seemed as if he was saying the same thing over and over, repeating the inane fact that this had happened to his parishioners at the Saint John's Episcopal Church in Chew's Landing, Gloucester Township, in the County of Camden, in the State of New Jersey, and that we should pray for world peace, yes, but we should also pray for our enemies, pray for our soldiers in Vietnam, pray for the innocent, for the guilty. It was endless and irrelevant, and it lasted far too long."

It wasn't until eleven-thirty that the funeral procession began its complex organization—taking another half-hour—then left the mortuary for the burial site behind Saint John's Church, using back streets to avoid the probing eye of the television cameras, only to come upon a sight that was more repellent than any of them could imagine.

Dozens of cars were parked along all the roads leading to the old church, creating a traffic problem that would add to the delay. It appeared to Bernie that hundreds of people had gathered there, strange-looking people, "the kind of people you don't see around Blackwood, dirty-looking kids, long-haired and sloppy, kids with beards and beads and sandals. They were scattered and grouped all over the cemetery, sitting on gravestones, trampling on flowers. Some had climbed nearby trees and roosted on branches for what they must have thought was going to be a spectacle. Some of them had cameras suspended from their necks like tourists. I swear I saw one lady in slacks who was actually picking up artificial flowers, stealing from other graves, perhaps looking for some souvenir to take home with her. And, of course, the television cameras were there. . . ."

It completely violated the Badiali image of propriety. There was nothing in their experience that could bring them to understand, much less respect, the sight of it, and Bernie became fearful of the responses of his father. He had had some presentiment of an eruption: his father had long been outspoken about such things. ("Long hair alone would drive him wild at times.") His uncles had similar proclivities and were, presumably, equally unpredictable in such weird, offensive situations. ("Suddenly I remembered a time when I was in college, in Brevard, N.C., and a friend of mine had a baby who died a few days after birth. I was a pallbearer at the funeral and I saw more grief than I'd ever seen before. I would have nightmares about the father jumping into the grave to be with his baby. And now I didn't know what was going to happen. . . .") Bernie had asked NBC's Rafael Abramovitz not to cover this scene, for if there should be an outburst, he could not bear the thought of its being recorded on film and Abramovitz had respected his plea and kept his crew away. But CBS was there and there was nothing anyone could do about it.

The family gathered around the grave and the Reverend Brace, now cloaked in a green shawl, covered the casket in green. This in itself was shocking to Bernie, who had assumed that red was the color of martyrdom. ("I'd wanted Craig to be honored with red, though I didn't really know enough about Episcopalian ritual to contest this.") Brace's final eulogy was far less wordy, but significant for its rejection of Craig's final message to the world. The Reverend Brace would later release a statement to the press as to his interpretation of the suicides: ". . . Were Joan Fox and Craig Badiali martyrs? I think that all of us should leave that sorrowful matter in the hands of God. Indeed, all of us should take this tragic matter in prayer to God. We should all take this whole sorrowful matter in frequent, earnest, and sincere prayer to our Lord and Saviour Jesus Christ. Can a resurrected good come from the tragic deaths of Joan

Fox and Craig Badiali? Yes it can and yes it will. But the extent of it depends upon all mankind. There will never be peace between man and man until there is godly peace between all men and God.

"Do you really want true and godly peace? Well, pray for God's peace again and again and again."

And then, from John, 16:33: "These things I have spoken unto you, that in me ye might have peace. In the world ye shall have tribulation: but be of good cheer; I have overcome the world."

Frank DiGenova, home for the funeral from Rensselaer Polytechnic Institute, was the only friend of Craig's who knew one of the letters had been written to him. ("My life is complete except all my brothers are in trouble—war, poverty, hunger, hostility. My purpose is to make them understand all this trouble. Maybe they will start a chain reaction of awakening, love, communication. . . .") Frank had seen those words in the Camden *Courier-Post,* not in Craig's hand. He told Thom Akeman after the funeral: "He said that people are the most important thing about life. He always had a lot of people who would take problems to him. He tried so hard to understand them. . . . He wrote out everything that bugged him. He just spent his time with people trying to make everybody else see how wonderful it is just to be alive. He saw a lot of beauty that he wanted everybody else to see. . . ."

Joan's brother Raymond was back from the service for the funeral of his sister on the following day, and the Reverend Brace said much the same thing. Her body was placed side by side with Craig's as they had requested. There were more flowers placed on her grave, and many of her friends were invited. Gail Hillias remembered that when Craig had taken Joan to the Ring Dance in December 1968, when the Junior Class received their rings, Joan wore a pink dress. Craig, who never seen her in pink, was dismayed, and Joan promised him that she would never wear pink again. Said Gail: "Joan was buried in a pink dress."

Stanley Pietrowski was there, too, as well as his opposite, Dennis Stewart, the boy who had adored Joan through these last few years. "He was very upset," Stanley said. "I guess he'd really been in love with Joan. I knew he didn't think much of me, the jock-versus-the-artist bit and all that. I was sort of sorry for him, the way he was grieving and all, but then he mumbled something, how it was all Craig's fault, that Craig had led her into this. Then he said something about how he was going to spit on Craig's grave. Well, I wasn't going to let him do that. So I told him, right there at the funeral scene, that if he did, I'd punch him right in the mouth. . . ."

Thus the ceremonies were ended. Later there were those who came to leave a final message, many who dropped more flowers on the grave, and one who left a peace sign, the inverted Y in a circle. It was this sort of "pagan" symbol that proved so annoying to the Reverend Brace, and when he learned of it, he returned to the grave and removed it.

20

In the early evening on Wednesday, a week after the suicides, the Quemores' reconverted barn was crowded with about twenty-five boys and girls who felt the need to memorialize their two friends. Mrs. Betty Quemore was impressed by their presence: "I knew of others who wanted to be here, but were afraid. Their parents had objected. They were shy of what others might say. I suppose some just didn't think they could measure up to the emotion of this sort of clandestine service."

It was a chilly evening, a sudden turn toward winter, and the breeze blew the fallen leaves in swirls around the spacious area behind the barn. They all gathered outside for the ceremony, carrying candles held close to their bodies to shelter them from the wind. Chief Quemore and family had set up a P.A. system to amplify the proceedings. Charlie Kean, the Highland graduate who had been en route to New York when paged in the bus terminal, presided. He told them all what an uncommon person Craig was, how lovely was Joan, and how much he, Charlie, had come to understand about himself as a result of knowing them. Desi played guitar and sang several of their favorite songs: "Blowin' in the Wind," "Where Have All the Flowers Gone?," "The Great Mandala." Her voice, at first gentle and lyrical, suddenly filled with emotion, so much so that on "Flora" she eventually cracked, taking others along with her. Stanley Pietrowski went inside and found a Bible, read a passage from Isaiah:

> And he shall judge among the nations, and shall
> rebuke many people: and they shall beat their
> swords into ploughshares, and their spears into

pruning hooks: nation shall not lift up sword against
nation, neither shall they learn war any more.

Charlie Kean read the equally well-known chapter of
Ecclesiastes:

To every thing there is a season, and a time to every
purpose under the heaven:

A time to be born, and a time to die; a time to
plant, and a time to pluck up that which is planted;

A time to kill, and a time to heal; a time to break
down, and a time to build up;

A time to weep, and a time to laugh; a time to
mourn, and a time to dance;

A time to cast away stones, and a time to gather
stones together; a time to embrace, and a time to
refrain from embracing;

A time to get, and a time to lose; a time to keep,
and a time to cast away;

A time to rend, and a time to sew; a time to keep
silence, and a time to speak;

A time to love, and a time to hate; a time of war,
and a time of peace.

And then he said that he believed it was their time to
live, and to live in a way that what Craig and Joan had
died for would not be in vain. And finally, there was a
Catholic priest, Father John, from Saint Jude's in Blackwood. He led a prayer in which he indicated no dis-
taste for the suicides of the two however it might have
violated Catholic ideology. His plea was for peace, human peace, and he openly condemned the war, and
because of who he was, it lent a special truth to the
ceremony.

It was lovely, this hour of tribute, unlike anything any

of them had ever experienced before, an improvisation
of their own for the memory of two of their own; an
hour without artifice or show of special ritual.

It was, nonetheless, something less than complete.
They stood there at its ending, cold and sad and unre-
quited. There was still too much left unsaid, too many
people left outside the pale of this experience, too many
questions still to be answered. They had come out of
loyalty and devotion, but in their minds there was too
much confusion. They wanted to believe and to say they
could understand the meaning of this tragedy, that for
all its sadness there was beauty in its intent, that Craig
and Joan had not died in vain. But they knew it would
not be that simple. Too many people would ask it, over
and over. Why? Why did they do it? Why? Why?

And there would be no way to tell them all a really
convincing answer.

There was another memorial service that evening. The
announcement read: "IN MEMORIAM Craig and Joan.
Tonight at 8 o'clock. Epiphany Lutheran Church. 7th
and Market Streets Camden. Bring a Candle. . . . they
are not alone in silence."

This was the call of Father Robert Oberkehr, or
Father Bob, as he was affectionately called by the several
hundred kids who gathered at the basement of his church
on Wednesday and Friday evenings. "The Door's Open,"
it was called. The minister was younger than the Reverend Brace, a mid-Westerner by origin, a lover of
people by nature. He was a tall, well-built man, but his
bright reddish beard and hair and the glasses that
covered his twinkling, friendly eyes made you less aware
of his physical style. Of all his weekly duties, these semi-
weekly gatherings were the most joyous for him, for
here were loving kids, grasping for some place to make
contact with each other and know that they were being
heard. He let them have it all, the entire room was
theirs, and they painted the walls with their own pop-
artistry, inscribing their message to the world in verse
and graffiti like young rebels on tenement walls.

"If you like Vietnam, you'll love World War III."
"Fighting for peace is like balling for virginity."

They would come to sing, dance to recordings, drink Cokes and eat homemade cookies and brownies, and sit at Father Bob's feet as he led them into the arts of communicating with each other.

He had never seen Craig and Joan, nor they him, but he had heard enough of their secret. It was the same with the hundred others who came that night.

The Quemore kids came, along with Desi, Stanley, and John Millet (who had never been there before). They had told Craig and Joan of these gatherings. "Sooner or later, they would have come," Stanley said. Others came tonight out of hunger for this one final moment of ceremony, Craig and Joan's friends in a roomful of strangers.

They sat on the floor, and Father Bob, in his unministerial garb, lit a candle and passed it to Desi, who lit hers from it, then on to Liz, to Stanley, and around the room in silence and in tears. They played records and some of them sang. Camden *Courier-Post* columnist Stephen Allen noted the songs and poems by which the kids made communication on that night while behind them all, NBC television cameras hovered to record it all. Some, like Liz Quemore, hated the presence of TV. To others, it added significance to the ceremony, a sense of its widespread importance that supplemented their own reverence. They were kids and suddenly the entire country would now be watching them.

> You're right from your side
> And I am right from mine;
> We're just one too many mornings
> And a thousand miles behind.
> —Bob Dylan

"It was lovely in that room," said Liz. "The candles and the singing and the sadness. I began to cry—I knew I would—and it was a special kind of crying, not just for Craig and Joan, but for all of us now. Here were all these kids who didn't even know them, but they knew what they meant, that we had all gotten to the point where we couldn't stand the horrors of the war and the way America was heading. I was crying because it all seemed so damn hopeless and it shouldn't be, because people are really so beautiful. . . ."

Why has this moment come
When childhood has to die?
When hope shrinks to a sigh
And speech into a drum?
Why are they pale and still?
                —Jacques Brel

"I was so damn tired emotionally," said Stanley, "it was like I couldn't see where my next breath was coming from. You think, it's really all so simple the way people should love each other and care enough about each other, at least to try, and that's what Craig and Joan wanted, that's really all there was to it. There, in that room with Father Bob and those kids, you felt that very deeply, nothing else makes much sense then, the violence in the world, the ugliness, racism and all, and then you know why Craig and Joan did it and it just kicked the hell out of you. . . ."

Ah, love, let us be true
To one another! for the world which seems
To lie before us like a land of dreams,
So various, so beautiful, so new,
Hath really neither joy, nor love, nor light,
Nor certitude, nor peace, no help for pain;
And we are here as on a darkling plain
Swept with confused alarms of struggle and flight,
Where ignorant armies clash by night.
                —Matthew Arnold

"I just get torn apart by gatherings like this," Desi said. "I saw Liz break down again—she just couldn't hold it in any more and she went running from the room, tears streaming down her face—and then John Millet, too. I was thinking of Joan, poor Joan, poor lovely Joan, she just didn't know that there was so much more love in the world than what she had seen in Blackwood. She really didn't know. Nobody really does in Blackwood. I thought, My God, if we could take the hundred kids in this room, candles and songs and feeling and tears, and surround Mr. Keegan, say, or a thousand Blackwood

parents who haven't the slightest idea what they are doing to the world, would it make a dent? Would it?"

> Some will come and some will go
> We shall surely pass
> When the wind that left us here
> Returns for us at last
> We are but a moment's sunlight
> Fading on the grass.
> Come on people now.
> Smile on your brother,
> Everybody get together
> And love one another
> Right now.
>   —Chet Powers

Stephen Allen was deeply impressed. There were no
speeches, no sermon, he noted. For the most part, the
boys had long scruffy hair, some even bearded, dressed
in tattered jeans and sandals, and the girls seemed very
much in the same mode. Yet "no one tried to turn the
simple service into a 'peace demonstration.'" He, too,
noted the presence of NBC's television cameras. In ". . . the
curious 'media age' in which we lived, the reverence
and sincerity of the service probably will be much more
apparent on television than it was in reality. . . . We live
in strange times."

> All we are saying is
> Give peace a chance . . .
>   —The Beatles

On Thursday, a week after the tragedy, the Blackwood
Observer's weekly issue devoted its lead editorial to
summing it all up. They ". . . must have realized that
their deaths would accomplish nothing, just as the forty
thousand lives that they died in protest of accomplished
nothing. The real sorrow is the waste of two dedicated
youths, who if given the right direction, would have undoubtedly accomplished much. . . . Who do we blame?
We don't know, and like so many people who knew
Craig and Joan, we can only ask the question. . . . Why?"

Was this, then, the final evaluation: No one to blame; senseless waste; a large unanswerable question?

As Father Bob put it: If you keep asking a simple question over and over, people will believe there is no answer and then the question itself becomes a lie. "The answer was simple enough; all one had to do was look in his heart. . . ."

And therein lay the postscript to the tragedy. Except for family and friends, there was no soul-searching, no confession of responsibility, not even a public show of grief. As Stephen Allen put it: "In the small business center, through the streets and in the stores, there was little evidence that a town was in mourning.

"If a policeman had been killed enforcing the law, there would be black bunting everywhere, and all the flags would be at half-staff.

But there was not an inch of black anywhere. There was no indication in any of the store windows that they mourned the passing of two of their young who died in the name of peace.

"The Stars and Stripes fluttered proudly at the very top of the flagpoles around town; none of them was at half-staff. And even in front of Highland Regional High School . . . the flag fluttered at the top of staff. No outward sign of mourning . . ."

Nor was there any discussion of it at school, not during the week that followed their deaths or the days thereafter, not by teachers or administrators, and after a while, not by students either. At one point, the Reverend Brace was led to believe that he was to speak at the school assembly in his capacity as pastor to the two families, his message ostensibly to give meaning and interpretation to their deaths. It was as if the school authorities were thus intending to nullify any criticism of their official silence. But in the end, they decided against it, presumably out of respect for the families' sustained bereavement, and the presence of Joan's sister Ruth, a freshman. Whether or not they questioned the Reverend Brace's position as to the suicides was never disclosed.

The silence that followed the burials was pervasive, supported not only by the authorities, but by many of their friends as well. Mrs. Diane Wagner, out of genuine grief, continued to refrain from comment. Bill Billhardt, Mark Bunzell, Tom Bye, John Millet, and others, all deeply attached to the two, mostly gravitated toward the notion that there was nothing to be gained by any further references to the suicides just as there had been nothing gained by the suicides themselves. The quicker everyone could return to their normal lives, the better.

The NBC crew, harassed by obstacles and a blatant lack of official cooperation, frustrated by the resulting coolness of others, finally decided to abandon the documentary. They disappeared on Thursday, a week after the news first broke, and they did not return. Their film footage was never publicly shown, finally relegated to some storage shelf in a distant warehouse.

And so it was throughout the community. If the twenty-four suicide letters still remained at large—and no one seemed to know who had them (some said they'd been impounded by the county prosecutor's office; others heard they had been burned)—no one volunteered any efforts to secure them either by pressure or threat of litigation. The Reverend Brace, meanwhile, did some letterwriting of his own, seeking to explain his position in this nationally publicized tragedy to such duly-elected officials as his Congressman, John Hunt of the First District of New Jersey, Senator Clifford Case, and President Richard M. Nixon himself. The gist of his message was that the Moratorium was a left-wing plot to destroy young people's faith in God and America; that the Students for a Democratic Society was probably involved; that these forces warped the thinking of two sensitive children and drove them to this unfortunate position that, in turn, drove them to eventual suicide. He himself endorsed the President's Vietnam stand as did the overwhelming majority of the people in his community and believed that Nixon's policy was the best way toward a peace that Americans could be proud of. Above all, he believed that the only real peace was God's peace, and therein lay the true hope for the survival of the free world. In reply, he received a grateful and supporting letter from Congressman Hunt, and a polite if critical note from New Jersey's Senator Case who, as the Reverend Brace explained, was known to be a dove. (It is

not known if there was any comment from the White
House.)

It was a silence that was endlessly oppressive to some,
and kids like Desi would occasionally erupt in a burst of
anger at another's lack of concern. And Liz Quemore
would spell it out thus: "I don't understand all the silence, all the suppression of this thing. Nobody wants to
talk about it or discuss it, or let us get it out into the
open. If this thing was all so terrible, it should be exposed as such, shouldn't it? Why is nothing ever explained?" And Stanley, wearing his own frustration behind a mask of whimsy would say: "Craig had burned
all his papers the night before he died. All the things he
had written, poems and stories he didn't want anyone to
see. One would think he wrote those letters because that's
what he wanted the world to know, just those letters,
but they won't let us have them!"

And those who suffered above all, the Foxes and the
Badialis, could not help but sustain their grief, isolating
themselves as much as possible in a silent plea for
anonymity. Whatever troubled afterthoughts and questions and self-reappraisals they had remained discreetly
within the walls of their homes. If there was little
socializing between the two families before the suicides,
there was less afterward. It could be said that neither
knew quite what the other was thinking, and though they
might have wondered, it was not their way to stir such
troubled waters.

Through the long weeks of their bereavement, they
were warmed by hundreds of cards, letters, and flowers,
messages of support from all over the country. In the
Badiali living room, Craig's picture stands prominently
on the television console beside Bernie's. Another of
Joan is nearby. On the wall, a large oil painting by one
of Dolly's sisters views the fine old Saint John's Episcopal
Church from the very site of the two gravestones. One
senses the need to face their sustained anguish, never
pretending to conceal it through all their daily involvements.

Raymond Fox, nineteen, returned to service without
making any comments to the press or to anyone else.
The older son, Andrew, Jr., twenty-seven, went on with

his duties on the Gloucester Township Police Force and his own family life—as did Joan's oldest sister, Myrtle. Linda, twenty-one, was a working girl and would remain at home until her marriage in the early spring of 1970. Ruthie, fifteen, closest to Joan in age and sensitivity, would suffer the most. And outside the Fox home, the large American flag remained visible on the front porch.

It was much the same with the Badialis. Bernie, Jr., alone, had spoken out briefly on that tortured day after the suicides. He had returned to school at Glassboro State College to finish his education, preparing himself for a teaching career, while his wife took care of their baby son. Yet the tragedy of his brother's death ate away at him, forestalling any return to normalcy and tranquillity, demanding something of him, he knew not what —something that would make it all seem less than a tragic waste, something that would leave his brother's name in dignity. More than anyone else, he had been caught by the conflict inherent in the need for silence as opposed to Craig's quest for martyrdom and he could not free himself of it. His father, meanwhile, returned to work, a master carpenter and a foreman of a construction unit in Philadelphia or wherever an assignment might send them. Dolly Badiali's grieving continued to dominate the household, though not in any demonstrative way. The Reverend Brace was a daily visitor for weeks following the deaths, continuing to serve as a source of comfort to her.

There were, however, curious moments of embarrassment revolving around a bottle of Schenley's whisky that appeared frequently on the kitchen table for those who needed it. Dolly, who seldom touched a drop in her life, was pouring herself a small shot on the advice of her husband one afternoon when Brace burst into the room. Curiously, it happened again on the following day, and on the third, when she was not drinking, the bottle was nonetheless there in front of her, half empty now. For all her grief, the thought suddenly entered her mind that he must see her as a drinking woman, an image she found particularly distressing. The pattern, however, seemed unbreakable, for on a subsequent day, he burst into the house just as she was about to put the bottle

away. She found herself trapped in what had to be an
incriminating tableau, knowing that he would be inside
the kitchen well before she could get rid of the bottle
and think all the worse of her for her apparent attempt
to hide it. She just stood there holding it, like a child
caught with a hand in the cookie jar. The way he looked
at her—she would remember that for a long time.

Bernie, meanwhile, became increasingly annoyed by
Brace's presence.

"I couldn't help it; I began to question him about his
theology. I'd spent those years at Brevard College in the
heart of the Bible Belt, where some of the greatest
theologians in the country would visit and lecture, really
serious students of religious thought. To them, God was
not a big man up in the sky with a vast white beard.
I developed an intellectual sense of what religion ought
to be. I actually feel that I joined the church down there.
One thing was sure, I had learned something, and when
I confronted Brace, a man who posed as God's emissary,
I could challenge him. 'You may call me Father,' he
would say, like one must be respected simply because he
wore the cloth. I couldn't feel that, though. All I could
see was a man who had used the cloth to violate my
brother's death. He kept talking in terms of Craig and he
didn't even know him. Now he was working on my
mother, giving her remission for all her sins, luring her
back into the church. So I found myself challenging his
theories. I would talk about Malcolm Boyd, for example, a minister who I felt was really with it. *Are You
Running with Me, Jesus?*, Boyd's book, made Brace uneasy. 'I don't know what the clergy is coming to,' he
would say—and that the title ought to read Am *I* Running with *You*, Jesus? He hated Boyd for his liberalism
and was appalled that Boyd should submit to an inter-
view with *Playboy* magazine. Brace would say, If Jesus
was not in your life, you'd go to Hell, and that it was so
written. And I would answer, What about the hundreds
of millions of Africans who had never been Christianized? Hell would have to be terribly overcrowded,
wouldn't it? This competitive premise of his really galled
me, especially since it was opposite to what Craig believed: the relentless battle over good versus evil, of

God versus the devil, of devotion versus sin. It was the kind of repressive thinking that could be terribly destructive to the human psyche, keeping a person at war with himself and with others, for it thinks of people as essentially evil. Craig really hated that. . . ."

"Craig and I used to talk about religion," Steve Karras remembered. "He wondered about the whole thing to do with religion. He couldn't understand what good it had done in the world since there was all this war and inhumanity and poverty, and he felt that the church didn't really care about that. It cared only about whether you believed in God and contributed money, and if you did, the minister would bless you and you could go home feeling pure, you wouldn't have to contend with anyone's suffering anywhere.

"That was the whole trouble, he said. People felt pure without doing anything. They were told that they were all sinners anyway, that war was God's punishment for their sins, and that if they wanted peace they should find it in God and everything would be all right then.

"He was really serious about the problem. A lot of kids go around saying they're agnostics, or even atheists. They think it's cool to put down religion and all. But they're just winging it, like deep down inside they're apologizing to God. Not with Craig, though. If he found a religion that he felt really cared about people, he'd probably become a minister. . . ."

"The point is," Bernie said, "Craig saw that people can't go around pious and holy and God-fearing in the old way while they avoid caring about each other. The Christian ethic is supposed to be a love ethic, not a vague hope ethic in life-after-death. People should essentially live in the present with love for each other. They should find their God through love, not love through God. ('He who does not love does not know God': 1 John 4:8.)

"So I challenged Brace about these old-fashioned Fundamentalist concepts such as the virgin birth and transubstantiation. At first my parents would hear me say these things to him and be horrified. It was blasphemy, the way they saw it; I might as well have taken the cross and thrown it against the wall. But, after a

while, they began to think about it and even Brace would
have to admit I had a point now and then. He saw I was
not blabbing out of prejudice or ignorance, that I really
knew what I was talking about.

"When I'd leave the room, though, my parents would
say to my wife, 'What's gotten into Bernie? What is this
change in him?' And one night, it got to be a big scene.
My parents started to get to my wife, and she tried
to get me to stop this thing, and I had to defend myself
against her, too. It was like a wedge had been driven
into the family, all because of Reverend Brace. I guess
I exploded that night, and we all had it out. I said, 'Is
that your idea of a Christian?' 'But he's a son of God,'
they replied. I told them, 'No, he's just a man, he's not
God, he's not religion, he's just a man!'

"Well, they began to change after that. I could feel
that I'd made an impression. My wife finally agreed
with me, especially after we went to church to hear him
speak again.

"My mother even grew accustomed to my challenging
him. One night, weeks after the funeral, my brother-in-
law came over, Charlie Trocolli, an artist who'd graduated Montclair College. We were just sitting around
drinking beer and joking, and I began to tell him about
Reverend Brace, the arguments we'd had and all, and
how you just couldn't believe this man—and suddenly,
there he was, like a rabbit walking across the path of a
hungry man. I offered him a glass of wine, thinking it
was appropriate, but he saw us drinking beer and said
he'd prefer that. It was about nine o'clock when we began talking and we went at it hammer and tong. He
didn't leave until maybe one-thirty. We really laid it on
him, Charlie and I, and his head must have been spinning. My mom, she sat through it all, and I could tell
that she understood what was happening without letting
it bother her at all. It was a very satisfying night.

"We didn't see him for a while after that. He would
speak to my mom, though, and in the last analysis, I
guess he got what he wanted: she consented to be con-
firmed by him, a big thing for her to do and a big con-
quest for him."

(A double victory, perhaps, for it happened exactly a

month after the suicides, on November 15, the day of the largest peace demonstration that Washington, D.C., had ever seen.)

"Dad, meanwhile, continued to serve as vestryman in Saint John's. Whatever he might have felt about Brace, he chose not to make waves."

Months later, while gathering material for this book, Bernie visited the Reverend Brace, requesting copies of the sermon on the Sunday after the suicides and the eulogy delivered at the funeral, hoping they could be quoted *in toto*. Brace was both pleased and threatened by the prospects. His indecision of the moment was reflected in his argument that he felt uneasy at contributing to a work that might seek to make martyrs of the two.

Bernie wrote of their subsequent colloquy:

"You see," he said, "legitimate martyrs do not take their own lives."

"What about the Buddhists who burned themselves?" I asked. I also suggested that Jesus Christ himself knew he would be killed before he went into Jerusalem.

This offended him, I saw. In reply, he suggested that I was like those others who wanted to make a martyr of Martin Luther King "when actually he was just asking to be shot."

"What about Spiro Agnew or Billy Graham?" I argued. "Aren't they too asking to be shot?"

Again, I saw that I'd offended him.

He told me that he was worried that such a book as this might influence other kids to kill themselves in the name of peace. "A work like this might drive them off the edge," he said.

"It could also help some of them. It might give new understanding to their lives," I countered.

Then he tried a new tack: if he gave me the sermon it might be a mistake to take such a stand on behalf of the parish. "After all, the sermon was delivered to them, for their benefit. Besides," he tried to conclude, "the Fox family have not given their consent to the writing of this book and I feel a responsibility to them too. . . ."

"But my mom and dad are just as much a part of the parish. You have an equal obligation to them."

He had the habit of putting his thumb and forefinger to his chin as he began to nod, admitting that he was, indeed, perplexed about to whom the sermon actually belonged. Then he admitted that Jesus was in a somewhat similar situation: when the elders brought money to Him, asking Him to tell the people what to do with it, Jesus said: "Give to Caesar what is his. . . ." And suddenly, the prospects of his turning over the material seemed very much improved. I even thought that his eyes were shining in a special way, and it occurred to me that he would enjoy the prospect of being so prominent in a book where his sermons would be quoted.

I was surprised, then, when he called me two days later and told me that he would *not* give me the sermon, and he added that, as my pastor (which, of course, he isn't), I should stop assisting the writer on the entire project.

And so, it appeared, Bernie's extended confrontation with the Reverend Brace came to an end. He would take stock of it from time to time, especially in the company of his parents who had never approved of the controversy. On one occasion, it was mentioned that Craig— over whom the entire issue was mounted—would not have approved either, that his way would have been a gentle way, a search for mutual compassion and understanding. Craig would never have challenged him.

Bernie saw this and knew it was true. He had seen what he had considered to be the reverend's violation of

Craig's death, but Bernie himself, in the power of his resentment, had somehow compounded that violation. It would move him to think again how beautiful was the love ethic that his brother had come to live by.

The silence of his community did not sit comfortably with at least one of the silent. Craig's friend Steve Karras had gone along with it all, saying nothing to challenge any of it, not even pressing for that candlelight march. He spent his days doing his homework, playing in the school band, listening to records, dating two girls and thinking about a third, and wondering when he would no longer have to face his acne.

His troubles began during the weekend of the November 15 peace demonstration in Washington, a family time around the early evening news. On television, Steve watched the tremendous crowd of young people marching through the streets, suddenly sensing, for the first time in his life, that this had something to do with him. If the marchers were shown to be as dirty and hippie-like as one might expect, it no longer bothered him that much. He couldn't explain it; he didn't even understand his emotion. It might even have disappeared, a transitory reaction no more consequential than the smell of a chocolate cake baking through a neighbor's kitchen window. But then his father shattered his tranquility. "I tell you, these kids are out to destroy this country!"

"I didn't say anything. I guess I was too confused. I mean, I always thought my father and I pretty much agreed about things. But this seemed like a slap in the face. It was like he was saying that about Craig.

"I thought about that a lot, I guess. I wanted to talk about it with him, but somehow I couldn't. Not yet, anyway. It ended up, I had to talk about it with someone else first.

"It just happened to be with Stanley. I always thought of him as a weirdo, though I could see why Craig might like him. I mean, he was okay. We just happened to sit together at lunch one day, and it happened. I guess I provoked him into it, saying something about how maybe it was best that everyone had sort of forgotten about the suicides by then. Stanley jumped all over me.

" 'It's not best at all,' he said. 'It's the worst thing. Most people are ashamed of it. The whole town is ashamed of it. They won't admit the two died for peace, it sounds too unpatriotic for them. If Craig and Joan had done this thing on July 4 instead of Moratorium Day, and if those letters said they were dying because of super-patriotic reasons, like there wasn't enough respect for the U.S. flag or they were protesting against all the radical-perverted-bearded hippies, you could bet this town would be rocking with brass band memorials, playing taps at parades with flags at half-mast all over the place! . . .'

"I thought, wow, I'd never thought of that.

"I saw him again a few days later and he was talking about the letters that Craig and Joan had written. He was telling about how he'd heard that Reverend Brace had written a letter to the President explaining the whole suicide thing, how it really bugged him because he had the idea that Craig had written one to the President, too, but Craig's was sitting somewhere in Police Chief Jones's house. Craig had killed himself for peace, but the letter that gets to the President is written by a man who believed in the war!

"It didn't seem fair, no matter how you looked at it. The whole thing began to bother me a lot. It got so I began to have trouble sleeping, I mean, it stuck in my mind. Those letters, they really bothered me. After a while, it even frightened me, the way I'd have fantasies about them, right in the middle of class or something. And one morning, real early, I woke up sweating and feverish and sick: I had this dream, a real crazy dream, that I went to *steal* those letters!

"It was only a dream, but a few days later I knew I was really going to do it. When Christmas vacation began, I actually began to plan it. It was crazy—I'd never stolen a thing in my life—but I had to do this. I started going over to where Chief Jones lived, just to look it over, like in the movies, casing the joint. I got to know the house and how they moved in and out of it, and when the door was most likely to be open, when there'd be no one home. I'd stand out there for an hour or so, and it was cold, too. I guess I'd really freaked myself out trying to get myself ready to do it. I got a flashlight, gloves to avoid fingerprints, a screwdriver to jimmy open a drawer if I had to. I mean, it didn't seem too wild—he probably had a den or something, a room for a home office of some kind. It probably wasn't even locked. The more I thought about it, the easier it seemed . . . a pile of light blue airmail envelopes, probably with a rubber band around them.

"Finally I thought I had the right time to do it. There was no one home. I'd actually seen them all leave.

"I walked up to the front door and no one was around to see me. At least no one I could see. And then, like an idiot, I rang the bell. There was no one home and I rang the bell, and I knew right then I couldn't go through with it. I was shaking all over, I was so nervous I don't think I could've picked my own nose.

"I went home and lay down on my bed. I even laughed at myself. I was sweating like mad despite the cold, so I took a long hot shower. My mother was worried, I think: me showering in the middle of the day like that. I didn't say anything and she didn't ask. Nobody said anything —which is strictly normal, I guess."

A few weeks after the suicides, Desi Worland became eighteen years old, and with it, she could legally free herself from the custody of the state and the stultifying confines of her foster home. Since her arrest and three months in prison, her life had been infinitely less than gratifying. "When I'd returned to Highland in September, they kept me in junior class. They said I never took exams last spring—which was true—but they never let me take a make-up exam like they promised I could. They even shoved me in freshman art, deliberately, just to humiliate me, it seemed. I tried to get Mrs. Wagner to help me, but she couldn't buck the authorities. So I took all the credits I could. I began to read every book in the library, practically, I just didn't want to be so damn bored with school."

Then her friend had died. She would drive by the cemetery, knowing those two stones were right there in front of the fence by the road, but she would shut her eyes as she passed. She had not been invited to the funeral ("I'd never once felt welcome in the Foxes'

house.") and spent that Tuesday morning in a kind of
grieving stupor that "seemed like the end of a bad trip."
In the days that followed, she raged too quickly at the
apparent ease with which her classmates and the school
could pass off this whole affair. Once, when a boy saw a
venal cartoon of kids carrying Viet Cong flags and linked
this to Craig and Joan, Desi erupted like a tigress, only
to be left with her futility in the resulting overloaded
silence.

Her friend was dead and hardly anyone seemed to
care. Her friend had died for them all, but it didn't
matter. Nothing had changed. Everybody had seen to
that. "That was the trouble: the kids had actually been
taught not to react. Whatever they might feel about anything, they had long ago learned not to say anything or
do anything because if you did, you might get into
trouble. So they didn't. They never said a word. They
were like dead."

Early in November she packed her battered suitcase
with clothes and a few choice books and, for the last
time, drove by the cemetery of Saint John's Episcopal
Church (once again averting her eyes) and on toward
the New Jersey Turnpike that would take her to New
York. She had no idea what she would do or how she
would survive. She was tired of grieving and suddenly
aware of her terrible fragility. (In fact, in two months,
she would be desperately ill with pneumonia in an East
Village cold-water flat.) And as the car finally took her
away, tears suddenly flooded her eyes, and all her
anguish and frustration and love and pain drove her to
one last moment of exasperation. She faced the Black
Horse Pike and its consummate ugliness and mumbled
her parting words: "God damn you, Blackwood!"

For all the others who remained, the autumn turned
into the long cold winter and the wind whipped across
the countryside as damp and biting as ever. There were
no noticeable changes in Gloucester Township as the
decade of the 1960s came to an end. The Highland
wrestling team was having another outstanding season
and the football team had lost its usual quota of games.
The highly touted marching band, requesting an invita-

tion to the New Year's Day Cotton Bowl festivities in Dallas, Texas, was accepted after the committee reviewed films of its prowess, and the community prepared itself for what promised to be a prideful adventure. In fact, State Senator Hugh Kelley had assured bandmaster Joseph DeMenna, *et al.*, that he would secure the five thousand dollars necessary to fly the entire band to Texas at the next meeting of the Jersey legislature. When his efforts failed, the kids and their parents canvassed the area to raise sufficient funds to rent buses for the fourteen-hundred-mile trip. The proud bandmaster, like a football coach predicting victory, told their ardent supporters that his was a band good enough to march with any band in the country. Indeed, of the eighteen bands at Dallas on that nationally televised sunlit day, the stirring words were telephoned back to Blackwood: "We're Number One!" It lifted the town right out of its postholiday doldrums. A huge welcome-home feast was immediately prepared under the auspices of the president of the Board of Education himself, Joseph Moffa, owner of the huge banquet hall called Moffa's Farms. A police escort was waiting for the bus caravan as it emerged from the Jersey Turnpike after thirty-six hours on the road, and the one hundred and forty-five weary young heroes were brought directly to their jubilant parents and one thousand proud Blackwoodians to celebrate their triumph at a roast-beef dinner in their honor. It was a gala occasion, replete with speeches by such dignitaries as State Senator Hugh Kelley, Congressman John Hunt, and Mayor Joseph Menna, topped by a huge cake honoring the triumphant band and especially its leader, Joe DeMenna. The Blackwood *Observer* featured the story in its subsequent issue on January 8: "HIGHLAND HIGH MARCHING BAND #1 IN COTTON BOWL COMPETITION," ran the lead headline.

However, there were bandmasters of neighboring communities who believed the award was suspect, having long since felt that the Highland band was hardly better than mediocre. And when the *Observer*'s intrepid young reporter, Carleton Sherwood, communicated directly with the head of the Cotton Bowl committee in Dallas, he received a reply that included the following revelation:

"There is no competition [of marching bands], and when we received a letter with clippings a few weeks ago, we were confused, to say the least. . . ." The *Observer* of January 22 pulled no punches in its exposure of the fraud: "RUMOR SPARKS HIGHLAND WIN 'MISTAKE' SAYS COTTON BOWL."

Significantly, it was not bandmaster Joe DeMenna (who, at best, had guilty knowledge of the deception) who came in for criticism; it was young Carleton Sherwood for its exposure. It also became known that when, in an earlier competition, DeMenna had let it be known that the band had been in the top ten, it had actually tied for last in a field of twenty-two. Nonetheless, most typical was the reaction of the cake-maker herself: "Win or lose, we're proud of you."

Sherwood said: "I guess people believe only what they want to believe."

There was another flurry of local excitement some months later when town officials suddenly "discovered" that many of their children were violating federal narcotics laws. A burst of police activity followed in a belated and futile attempt to repress this. There were the usual raids and arrests, cries of alarm and sermonizing. There were even police dogs, trained to sniff out marijuana, who were brought into schools and led along hundreds of steel lockers that lined the hallways, indicating to officers which to break into. "It was a challenge," said one student: "Some of us started to leave open cans of Ken-L Ration. . . ."

If the use of pot continued, it was the only show of defiance toward established authority, for Blackwood kids remained safely isolated from the rest of America's rebellious youth culture. When the April 15 Peace Mobilization once again sought to rally a nation-wide protest against the Vietnam War—exactly six months after the suicides of Craig and Joan—there was even less local enthusiasm for its demonstration than the scanty participation in the October Moratorium. In this regard, Blackwood reflected the growing backlash of the entire nation. If America was weary of that frustrating war, it was perhaps even more frightened at the prospect that its historical invincibility was at an end.

New York Times....
WASHINGTON, APRIL 15
A majority of Americans appear ready to restrict basic freedoms guaranteed by the Bill of Rights, according to a poll by the Columbia Broadcasting System. . . . Even with no clear danger of violence, 76% said they opposed the freedom of any group to organize protests against the government. . . .

The spring of 1970 was a time of counterdemonstrations by urban "hard-hats," the dangerous expansion of the war into Cambodia, killings of students by National Guardsmen at Kent State in Ohio, and a rising polarization of American political opinion repeatedly enhanced by the Administration's attempt to rally its Great (No-Longer-) Silent Majority of supporters.

"It's a time," said a Blackwood student, "when Craig must be turning in his grave."

For the most part, however, the suicides of Craig and Joan lay dormant in memory, no longer mentioned or discussed, a subject to be avoided and forgotten. As the Reverend Charles Brace put it: "The town wants it to die, if possible, to forget about it. It's a morbid memory which does no one any good. It was a sad sick thing . . . the parents suffered so . . . isn't it better to let the whole matter be buried completely? . . ."

New York Times
MAY 30
by James Reston
. . . The surprising thing about the appalling tragedies (800,000 killed in Vietnam, official Pentagon figures) is not that there are so many antiwar demonstrations, but that such a slaughter is accepted with such indifference. . . . The Pentagon is still talking about the "kill-ratio" in Vietnam and the "body-count" of enemy dead—two of the most offensive phrases in the history of warfare. . . . We cannot even decorate the graves of the dead this

Memorial Day, for we don't even know where most
of them are. . . .

The cemetery at the old Saint John's Episcopal Church
at Chew's Landing was the scene of a special baccalaure-
ate ceremony of the graduating class of Highland Regional High School. Almost forty students, friends of
Craig and Joan, chose to congregate there for a moment's thought, the first such organized recognition of
their deaths. The two graves, side by side ("like Romeo
and Juliet," they said), were covered with flowers, and on
the stones, the inscriptions touched them all:

JOAN FOX
"ALWAYS IN OUR HEARTS"

and

CRAIG BADIALI
"LOVE AND PEACE"

Bernard Badiali, Sr., was there with them (he did not
bring his wife), and stood in the background to watch
while the priest spoke briefly. He saw his son through the
eyes of his friends and, because of the simple beauty of
the occasion, felt closer to the meaning of his death. The
Foxes were also there.

On this very day, in Haverford, Pa., less than forty
minutes away, a beautiful seventeen-year-old high school
girl named Denise Richter hooked a vacuum cleaner
hose to the exhaust pipe of her family car, threaded it
through the rear window, and turned on the ignition.
Her body was found with a black armband on her sleeve.
It said: "STOP THE KILLING."